with

# BIRTH
# CONTROL

Michael D. Benson, M.D.

THE ROSEN PUBLISHING GROUP, INC./NEW YORK

YA
613.9
Ben
1998

Published in 1988, 1992, 1998 by The Rosen Publishing Group, Inc.
29 East 21st Street, New York, NY 10010

**Revised Edition 1998**

*Cover photo by Frank Priegue/International Stock*

**Library of Congress Cataloging-in-Publication Data**

Benson, Michael D.
    Coping with birth control/Michael D. Benson.
    Bibliography
    Includes index.
    Summary: Discusses various aspects of sexual activity and birth control for both male and female teens.
    ISBN 0-8239-2620-6
    1. Birth control—United States—Juvenile literature. 2. Contraceptives—United States—Juvenile literature. 3. Sex instruction for teenagers—United States—Juvenile literature. [1. Birth control. 2. Sex instruction for youth]. Title.
HQ766.8.B461988
613.9.0084.008024055—dc19                              88-23958
                                                                              CIP
                                                                              AC

*Manufactured in the United States of America*

## About the Author

Michael D. Benson received his bachelor of medical science degree and his M.D. from Northwestern University. His specialty training in Obstetrics-Gynecology was also done at Northwestern. He is now in private practice in the northern suburbs of Chicago and delivers babies at Highland Park Hospital, Highland Park, Illinois. He is the author of a book on obstetrics for doctors in training and has written more than a dozen papers and book chapters in medical literature.

Dr. Benson is especially interested in health education and preventive medicine. To this end he has developed a sex education program for junior high school children in Chicago. He has given lectures to thousands of children on motivation in school and sexually related topics. He has also developed a questionnaire for public school students to measure teen behavior relevant to health and education.

Dr. Benson lives with his wife, Bonnie, and his two children in Deerfield, Illinois.

# Contents

Preface   1

Introduction   3

*PART I - Your Changing Body*

1 Sexual Anatomy   7

2 The Menstrual Cycle   11

3 Adolescence   18

4 Pregnancy   24

*PART II - Contraception*

5 Is It Safe and Effective?   30

6 Abstinence and Periodic Abstinence   35

7 Oral Contraception   39

8 Norplant Contraception   50

9 Other Types of Hormonal Contraception   55

10 The IUD   58

11 The Condom   65

12 The Diaphragm and Cervical Cap   69

13 Spermicides   74

14 Abortion   77

*PART III - Sexually Transmitted Disease*

15  What Are STDs?    85

16  Specific Diseases    94

*PART IV - Questions and Answers About Sex*

17  Frequently Asked Questions    109

18  Sexual Knowledge Self-Test    117

Glossary    123

Where to Go for Help    125

For Further Reading    127

Index    129

# Preface

Early in medical school I had the chance to hold a tiny newborn infant in my arms. That was when I knew I wanted to become an obstetrician-gynecologist. The newness and innocence of such a young life was thrilling. No matter how many times I have witnessed births, I have never lost the excitement of seeing an infant come into the world. The joy of the parents and relatives spreads among the hospital staff. And unlike many other patients in the hospital, new mothers, for the most part, are overjoyed at their remarkable achievement—bringing a human being into the world.

As my medical experience grew and as I gained better perspective, however, I began to see the birthing experience in a different and not always joyous occasion. Many mothers were too young to take care of their children and were often unprepared to guide them through the many pitfalls of daily living. Nor did I see many fathers at the birth.

Becoming more involved in the obstetrical routines at the very large hospital where I trained, I saw teenagers hardly out of grammar school giving birth. The new mothers were often fearful and alone. They were seldom supported by the baby's father or close relatives. Looking into the eyes of new, too-early mothers, I regularly saw regret and bewilderment.

This book is a further extension of my concern at seeing so many young women having babies before they can properly provide for their care and financial support. The anguish and disillusionment that typically occur when an unmarried teenager has a baby can be forestalled in part by providing teenagers with sound information about their bodies, the sexual experience, and birth control.

Michael D. Benson, M.D.

# Introduction

Some teenagers think that having sexual intercourse is an important step toward becoming an adult. This is not true, it depends upon the circumstances under which the event occurs. Much like anything else in life, the significance of the sexual experience must be judged by the other events surrounding it. Driving for the first time, having a baby, getting married, or graduating from school do not of themselves make a person an adult.

While sexual intercourse is not of itself a mark of adult behavior, for many teenagers it can have devastating consequences that can affect the rest of their lives. It can serve to ruin their health and futures because of disease or pregnancy. Teenagers who decide to have sex need to be informed of the possible consequences of their actions—contracting sexually transmitted diseases (STDs), such as AIDS, or becoming pregnant when they aren't ready to be parents. In order to protect yourself from these consequences, you need to learn about how your bodies work. If you make the decision to have sex, learn about the different forms of birth control available to protect yourself.

To understand contraception (from two Latin words, meaning "against conception"), one must first understand conception, or how a baby is created in the first place. A baby is created when a couple engages in sexual intercourse but that is

not all there is to it—especially if sex is desired, but the partners do not want to have or are not ready for a baby. In the
chapters that follow I shall review sexual anatomy, the menstrual cycle, various methods of contraception, and some
dangerous diseases that can be transmitted through sexual
activities.

There are teens who engage in sexual activities in the
hope of conceiving a baby. Some boys want to father a
child to prove their masculinity. Sometimes young women
want to get pregnant so that they can have a little person
to love and keep them company.

Becoming a teen parent may seem like a glamorous,
adult thing to do, or you might think it can prove something or make up for whatever seems to be lacking in your
life, but a baby drastically changes your life. Most teens
are not prepared for the changes. Let us look at what actually happens to teens who have sex and then become
parents before they are ready.

The United States has one of the highest teen pregnancy rates of any developed nation in the world. About one
million girls become pregnant every year in the United
States. By the age of eighteen, one out of every four girls
will have been pregnant at least once.

Teenage parenthood can be a disaster for the parents,
the baby, and society at large. Compared to girls who wait
until they're older to have children, teen mothers are only
half as likely to finish high school. They are seven times as
likely to be poor. For those few who do get married, more
than half are divorced within two years. Teen mothers also
tend to have more babies than those who wait until later
in life to start a family. As a result of all these facts, the

young woman who becomes a mother in her teen years is more likely to be poor and single for her entire life. Those who manage to succeed have to overcome very difficult obstacles. Some teens do, but the vast majority do not.

Being a parent is a full-time job in itself. Babies and small children need constant attention and cannot be left alone for a minute. It takes a lot of energy and patience to take care of a baby. It also takes a lot of money to feed and clothe them.

Before you make the decision to have sex, think carefully about the pros and cons of your decision. Make sure it is your decision; don't let anyone force you to do something you're not ready to do. This book will teach you about your body and how it functions and will give you information about birth control to help you make decisions to protect yourself.

# PART I
# YOUR CHANGING BODY

# Sexual Anatomy

Knowing how your body functions will enable you to make better and smarter choices about your body.

## The Male Body

Men carry most of their reproductive organs outside of their body. The reason for this is because sperm production seems to take place best a few degrees below normal body temperature. By carrying the testicles in a pouch hanging outside of the body, they are kept slightly cooler than internal organs.

Sperm are produced in the testicles but are carried in the body for a minimum of three months or so before they are released. By remaining "in storage," they have a chance to mature in preparation for fertilization. Once formed in the testicles, sperm move to specialized tubes known as the epididymis. Here, final preparation takes roughly two weeks. Sperm cannot swim before entering the epididymis but are strong swimmers after leaving it.

With sexual arousal and ejaculation, the sperm are transported out of the body through the vas deferens. This is a tubing that carries the sperm up and back away from the scrotum and then down to the prostate gland. The prostate gland adds additional fluid to the sperm as they pass through and out the urethra or urinary tube. With an erection, a valve is activated that closes the bladder and prevents urine from reaching the prostate.

Semen is a mixture of sperm and fluid from the prostate. Other glands, such as seminal vesicles and Cowper's glands, add fluid along the way. This mixture is called the ejaculate and is ejected from the penis in spurts during orgasm. The average ejaculate contains 100 to 200 million sperm and would fill half a teaspoon. Only one single sperm out of the many millions is needed to fertilize an egg.

The scrotum, which contains the testicles, is a very thin muscular sac that hangs down between the legs. The left testicle usually hangs lower than the right. During sex the testicles are pulled up toward the body. The penis in its flaccid state usually measures between two and four inches and is about one inch in diameter. Men who are circumcised surgically remove the fold of skin over the top of the penis known as the foreskin. The top or head of the penis is known as the glans.

During an erection the veins in the base of the penis close, thus trapping blood that is pumped in by the arteries.

## Female Sexual Anatomy

The female sexual organs are mostly internal; the parts that are visible consist of the pubic hair and the lips, or labia, that cover the vaginal opening. There are actually two sets of lips, the labia majora, which are the larger outer covering, and the labia minora, which are just inside.

The labia majora start at the clitoris, which is a small bump filled with sensitive nerves just underneath the pubic bone. The urethra or urinary tube passes within an inch underneath the clitoris. Below the urinary tube is the open-ing of the vagina. Where the labia stop, normal skin starts and separates the vaginal opening from the rectum. This region is known as the posterior fourchette. Only two to three inches normally separate the vagina from the rectum. The anatomy can be described another way. If a woman lies flat on her back, the first structure between her legs, mov-ing from top to bottom, is the clitoris. This is followed by three openings; the urethra, the vagina, and the rectum (in order). At the opening of the vagina is a tough piece of skin called the hymen. It is this structure that tears during the first episodes of intercourse. This experience is usually some-what uncomfortable and often results in some bleeding. The hymen rapidly heals so that subsequent sex is not uncomfortable.

The vagina itself is lined by a pink mucus membrane sim-ilar to the lining of the mouth. The vaginal walls expand to accommodate the penis during sex. Normally, there is no actual space in the vagina since it is a collapsed tube. Bath water does not enter the inner portion of the vagina.

In my experience as a doctor, many women will not examine themselves with a mirror unless they are worried about a sexually transmitted disease. On the first glimpse of their own hidden anatomy, the irregular lumps and bumps that are normal may appear to be terribly abnor-mal. It is helpful for young women to examine themselves with a mirror at least once, just to get a general idea of their anatomy.

At the top of the vagina is the cervix, the opening of the uterus or womb. It can be felt by reaching all the way back into the vagina. This is the opening of the cervical canal, a passageway that allows menstrual blood to leave the uterus and sperm to enter the uterus from the vagina. Normally, the cervical canal has roughly the same diameter as a cotton swab and is about one and one-half inches long. During labor the cervix opens up to about five inches across to allow the baby to pass through the birth canal.

The uterus, or womb, is about half the size of a woman's clenched first. Attached to the cervix, it consists of muscle that grows to accommodate the baby. The uterus is actually hollow and is lined by specialized tissue, called the endometrium, that can provide nourishment to a developing baby. Attached to either side of the uterus are the fallopian tubes. About three inches long, they are the passageway for an egg to travel from the ovary into the uterus.

Ovaries lie behind and to the side of the uterus. It is here in the ovaries where the eggs are produced. The ovaries usually measure two inches long and one inch in diameter. They are suspended in the pelvis from above by the blood vessels that nourish them. It is not possible to touch the ovaries as they sit deep within the body and are not very big. In front of the uterus and ovaries lies the bladder. Behind and around these organs lie the small and large intestines.

# The Menstrual Cycle

Periodic vaginal bleeding in women is called the menstrual period, or period for short. Women have other names for monthly vaginal bleeding, such as "my friend" or the "curse." The time interval from the first day of one period to the first day of the next is known as the menstrual cycle. Women have varying degrees of fertility as the cycle progresses during the month.

## The Average Cycle

With the first day of vaginal bleeding, the woman's body has failed to detect a pregnancy in the preceding two weeks. As a result, the lining of the uterus, which had been growing thicker in preparation for a possible baby, is shed. It falls off the wall of the uterus, down and out through the cervix, and then out of the vagina, where it is visible as blood. This menstrual flow contains blood, the disintegrating egg, which is microscopic, and cells from the lining of the uterus, or endometrium.

The average menstrual flow is about four tablespoons of blood, although it often seems like more. While periods are typically of the same duration for a given woman, the days of bleeding among different individuals vary from three to seven days. The first day or so is usually the heaviest, and the flow tapers off toward the end of the period.

Menarche refers to the time when women have their first period. The average age of menarche in the United States is twelve. Most women start menstruating within three years of this age, or between ages nine and fifteen. The average time from the first day of one cycle to the first day of the next is twenty-eight days, although the normal range can be anywhere from three weeks to five weeks between menses for a given woman (an interval of twenty-one to thirty-five days). In the first two to three years after menarche, the menstrual periods usually occur irregularly, but a more regular pattern is soon established.

Menopause is the complete ending of the menstrual periods associated with a decline in female hormones in late middle age. In the United States the average age of menopause is fifty-one. It marks the end of a woman's ability to have children. There is no corresponding biological event for a man.

## Menstrual Discomfort

Most women experience a variety of symptoms with their periods including lower abdominal cramping, diarrhea, nausea, leg swelling, backache, and irritability. The nausea and pain come from the release within the uterus of a class of chemicals known as prostaglandins. A variety of medicines can block the production of prostaglandins and are thus effective in reducing discomfort and nausea. One such medication is ibuprofen, available in nonprescription form under several brands names, such as Advil®.

Women vary greatly in the type and severity of symptoms that accompany their periods. Some women have very light, easy-to-tolerate menses, whereas others are utterly disabled for a day or two. Again, medication is often of great benefit. If all else fails, the birth control pill is usually effective in making menstrual periods easier to tolerate. It is so helpful, in fact, that it is often prescribed for this reason even to women who have no other reason to seek contraceptive protection.

Most women have some type of premenstrual discomfort, and some women have more problems than others. Although cyclic discomforts can be quite disruptive, generally they are not symptoms of serious underlying disease. If you are concerned about your symptoms, or if they are so painful that they prevent you from participating in your normal day-to-day activities, speak to your doctor about it.

## Feminine Hygiene

Women typically use two methods to prevent menstrual blood from staining their clothes. The first is the sanitary napkin, or pad, which made up of several layers of soft cotton that absorbs liquids. The sanitary napkin is attached to the underwear between the legs and serves to absorb the blood released from the vagina.

The second method is the tampon, a narrow tube also made from cotton. A tampon is placed inside the vagina to absorb the blood and can be removed as necessary by pulling the attached string that hangs outside of the vaginal opening.

Tampon use will not cause a loss of virginity or increase the chance of disease.The only danger associated with tampons is the rare possibility of developing Toxic Shock Syndrome (TSS). The risks for TSS can be decreased by changing your tampons often and storing unused tampons in a clean and dry place.

## Fertility

The most important thing to remember about the menstrual cycle is the relationship of menses to maximum fertility. To understand this, it is necessary to describe what the ovary is doing at each point in the cycle. The first day of the cycle is the first day of vaginal bleeding. The end of that menstrual cycle occurs with the beginning of the next period.

In the first few days of the cycle, the ovaries begin producing increasing amounts of estrogen. This hormone serves to activate a dozen or so dormant eggs. As the individual eggs begin to mature, the cells around them secrete fluid. Thus, each egg is housed in a fluid-filled sphere within the first seven days of the cycle.

During the second week of the cycle, the largest egg continues to develop while the smaller eggs stop growing and eventually disintegrate. By the end of the second week, one egg is ready for release and is contained in a pool of fluid that is a minimum of one inch in diameter. The pool is popularly known as a cyst; physicians sometimes call it a follicle. When the cyst breaks open, the egg spills out of the ovary into the nearby fallopian tube, where it begins a two-day journey to the uterus. The release of the egg is known as ovulation and marks the beginning of a woman's most fertile days.

After ovulation the cells that had surrounded the egg then begin to produce another hormone called progesterone. This hormone helps stabilize the lining of the uterus in preparation for a possible pregnancy. If no pregnancy occurs, the ovary stops producing progesterone exactly fourteen days after ovulation. Without progesterone, the thickened lining of the uterus begins to break up and the menstrual period begins.

The first half of the menstrual cycle is called the follicular phase because it is when the egg in its follicle is prepared for release. It is this part of the cycle that varies from woman to woman. Once ovulation occurs and the egg is released, menses follows in twelve to fourteen days. This second half of the cycle, the luteal phase, almost never varies among women. As a result, a woman's highest fertility comes fourteen days before the next period. In women who have twenty-eight-day cycles, ovulation coincidentally also occurs fourteen days after the beginning of the last period. However, in a woman with a thirty-five-day cycle maximum fertility occurs twenty-one days after the first day of her last period. In a woman with a twenty-one-day cycle ovulation occurs on day seven.

This sequence unfortunately seems to cause endless confusion. Some of my patients think that they ovulate fourteen days after their period begins, while others think that they are most fertile fourteen days after it ends. Part of the mix-up arises from the fact that in the average twenty-eight-day cycle, fourteen days before the next period happens to be cycle day number fourteen. However, that is just coincidence. The key is to remember that the next period comes fourteen days after ovulation and that ovulation can happen at almost any time.

Can you predict when you will ovulate? Yes, but the prediction is no more than an educated guess. By determining the shortest and longest intervals between periods, you can narrow down the days on which ovulation is likely to occur. The accuracy of this guess is increased in those who plot out their periods for six months to a year and find that their cycle length does not vary much. Those with occasional cycle lengths of more than thirty-five days cannot predict ovulation with much reliability. It is important to remember that women on the birth control pill do not ovulate and that ovulation after any type of pregnancy is very unpredictable.

How long is the fertile period? It was previously thought that the sperm and egg can each survive for about two days. Therefore, the fertile period was stated to be for two days before and after ovulation. However, more recent evidence suggests that this may not be true. Rather, the latest thinking is that the fertile period begins 6 days before ovulation and ends with ovulation. Sex during this time can result in pregnancy.

If one were to take the discussion about ovulation quite literally, it might well be concluded that pregnancy is easy to avoid. After all, just avoid sex six days before ovulation. But, again, predicting the exact time of ovulation is not easy. In truth, most women have no symptoms when they ovulate. Also, even women with regular periods will usually have one irregular cycle every year. Since ovulation is difficult to predict, it is safest to assume that a woman is fertile any time after the third day of her cycle—virtually the entire month!

A few women do have experience symptoms of ovulation. This usually consists of a day or two of light vaginal bleeding in midcycle or one-sided pelvic pain that lasts from several hours to a day. Rarely, the pain of ovulation can be so severe that it is confused with appendicitis. Some women make the mistake of thinking that vaginal bleeding from ovulation is the start of their menstrual period. Such a miscalculation can result in pregnancy. Other women actually think that they are most fertile during their period and least fertile between periods. Of course, this error also puts unsuspecting women to the possibility at risk of getting pregnant.

## Important Facts to Keep in Mind

1. Women are most fertile midway between their periods—when there is no vaginal bleeding.
2. The least fertile time is during the period—a time when many couples do not want to have sex. Although, remember that a woman's menstrual cycle changes from month to month, making it difficult to predict when ovulation occurs and when it is "safe" to have sex.
3. A late menstrual period is often the first sign of pregnancy.

# Adolescence

When does a boy turn into a man or a girl into a woman? People have had many different answers to these important questions throughout the ages. It is a gross oversimplification to suggest that adulthood is achieved with the development of fertility. Becoming an adult has many facets, only one of which is the ability to be a parent. There is no single factor that makes a person an adult; rather, adulthood is the combination of many factors.

First, let us discuss some of the changes that a young person undergoes during puberty. Few subjects cause more concern or fascination for teenagers than their involuntary and quite strange bodily changes.

## Male Development

In discussing the average timing of events for both boys and girls, it is important to realize that the onset, duration, and sequence of developments in puberty may vary greatly from person to person. Indeed, the pattern described here is a composite of a very large group of teens. However, it cannot describe precisely what will happen to any one individual.

Most boys show some initial signs of puberty between the ages of nine and fourteen. As a rule, changes occur over a span of three years, although they can take as little as two years or as long as eight years completion. The first sign of puberty is usually the development of pubic hair along with an enlargement of the testicles. The voice then begins to crack, and armpit hair emerges. After this, the voice change becomes more pronounced and permanent. Accompanying the change in voice is a substantial growth spurt. Some teens will develop acne at this time. Pubic hair continues to grow and coarsen. Finally, one of the last changes for boys in their puberty cycle is the development of facial hair.

The first wet dream, or involuntary ejaculation during sleep, usually takes place within a year or so after the initial changes of puberty. For most boys, this occurs around age thirteen, an average of one year after girls have their first period. The sperm attain their adult concentrations and shapes in another twelve months. From a practical viewpoint, any young male who can ejaculate is able to become a parent and should use contraception if they engage in sexual activities.

## Female Development

As mentioned before, young women have their first period around the age of twelve. This event is not the first sign of puberty. On the contrary, it is really one of the last changes in female puberty development. As a rule, the first change is breast budding. This is not full breast development, but rather the growth of a small mound of tissue under the nipple. The next event is pubic hair growth followed by the presence of armpit hair. The peak of the hair growth occurs just after this point. The last main event is the menstrual period.

As puberty progresses, the initial changes become more pronounced. The onset of the first period does not indicate full fertility, since the cycles are usually irregular for the first year or two. It is possible (and it has happened) that a young woman can become pregnant even before her first menstrual period. As a result, there is no truly safe age at which a girl can have sex without risking pregnancy—even if she has not had her first period.

While medical science may not be able to explain why, a young woman's weight has a strong influence on the timing of her period. Thin athletes and girls who diet or don't eat correctly have delayed menarche and in extreme cases do not menstruate at all. The body requires a certain amount of fatty tissue to function properly.

## The Gynecological Exam

Although some may not consider this a relevant topic in a discussion of puberty, it is an issue about which many mothers and daughters have some concern. There are two main reasons for a teenager to see a gynecologist: anticipated sexual intercourse or the absence of a menstrual period by the age of sixteen. Teenagers who have regular menstrual periods and are not having sex do not have a strong need to see a physician. On the other hand, those who are having sex should see their gynecologist at least once a year even if they have no need for a birth control pill prescription. Sexually transmitted diseases and premalignant changes of the cervix are very real problems for teens engaging in sexual activities.

What takes place during a visit to the gynecologist? In general, the gynecologist will first take a medical history. Of particular interest to the doctor is the timing of the menstrual periods and the type of contraception used (if any). The doctor then does a general physical exam similar to that done by the pediatrician.

The only part of the experience that is difference from an examination by your regular doctor is the pelvic exam. With no rushing on the part of the physician, this examination takes roughly two minutes and should not hurt. It has three parts. First the doctor looks inside the vagina and at the cervix or the tip of the womb. This allows the doctor to take a Pap smear, in which he or she touches a cotton swab to the opening of the cervix and gently scrapes the cervix with a modified tongue depressor. The gynecologist uses an instrument called a speculum to separate the normally closed vaginal walls to see the cervix.

The second part of the pelvic exam is called the bimanual (two-handed) exam. The gynecologist places two fingers inside the vagina and the other hand on the lower abdomen. This enables him or her to feel the size of the uterus and the ovaries.

Finally, with one finger still in the vagina, the gynecologist places a finger in the rectum so that any abnormalities behind the uterus can be detected. With this step the two-minute pelvic exam is completed.

Virtually every teenager undergoing her first pelvic exam tells me, "It wasn't as bad as I expected." Of course, it can be quite intimidating, and people often imagine the worst. Fortunately, we doctors try hard not to live up to these fearful expectations. The exam usually takes less than two minutes and should not hurt.

Most doctors take the matter of patient confidentiality very seriously. Gynecologists, in particular, are careful

21

about discussing any aspect of a patient's care with anyone but the patient. As a rule, we do not answer the questions of curious mothers without obtaining the daughter's permission. For anyone who is concerned about this policy, it is easy enough to call the doctor's office anonymously before the visit to check their policy.

## Importance of the Pap Smear

The Pap smear is a routine part of most gynecologic exams and may well prove to be a life-saving part of the examination for some women. The Pap smear is a screening test for cervical cancer. "Precancerous" changes of the cervix and other mild abnormalities are quite common. These problems may disappear by themselves, but if ignored over several years, they can occasionally progress to actual cancer. Precancer itself is easily cured in the office.

The Pap smear procedure, as noted above, consists of gently scraping the cervix with a modified tongue depressor. The material so obtained is smeared onto a slide and sent to a laboratory where it is examined under a microscope. In this way, early abnormalities in the cervix are detected and then treated before they have a chance to develop into cancer.

## Summary

The teenage years indicate a time of change and of exploring new ideas about yourself and the world around you. You may be anxious or confused about these changes, but always keep in mind that that they are normal and everyone goes through them. It is normal, as you grow older, that you become aware of your own sexuality and have questions about it. Keep in mind that there are always people around who can help or just offer support. The important thing is to reach out for help to get answers to your questions. Those answers will help you to make wise decisions about your future.

# Pregnancy

The main purpose of this book is to give teenagers enough information so that they can avoid becoming pregnant. But what if they do? This chapter briefly reviews some important facts about pregnancy and then describes the consequences for those teenagers who become parents.

## Finding Out that You Are Pregnant

The most important first sign of pregnancy is a late or abnormal menstrual period. In sexually active women with regular menstrual periods, being overdue by a week or more strongly points to pregnancy. Women with irregular periods cannot rely on the lateness of the period to suggest pregnancy. An unusually light period may also be an indicator of pregnancy.

Home pregnancy tests are inexpensive, easy to use, and highly reliable. They cost ten to fifteen dollars and usually give a result within twenty minutes. Many people do not trust the tests because they are so cheap and easy to use. However, their cheapness is not the result of poor quality but of the substantial progress that has been made by medical science. In general, home pregnancy tests can confirm a pregnancy within one to seven days of a missed period. Some newer tests are able to give you results a day after intercourse. The longer a woman waits to have the test, the more reliable the result. Even if the first test shows no pregnancy, it should be repeated in one week if the menstrual period still has not occurred. A physician should be consulted if the period is two weeks overdue and no pregnancy is indicated by the test.

As accurate as pregnancy tests are, they are always an emotional experience. Understandably, most women feel quite intense about the results, whatever they are. The home test is easy to confirm by having another urine test at a doctor's office or a clinic.

Many women feel very different physically within two weeks of missing their period. Some have waves of nausea (with or without vomiting). Others have bloating, breast tenderness, or fatigue. These symptoms can be confusing, since many women also experience them just before their menstrual period. Most women have some symptoms associated with pregnancy, but a few have absolutely none. The discomfort, such as breast tenderness or nausea, is usually mild and disappears within three months.

Many women, particularly teenagers, are fooled by bleeding that occurs in early pregnancy, mistaking it for a menstrual period. Virtually any type of vaginal bleeding can occur during pregnancy, and women should be suspicious if a period starts late, ends early, or is unusually heavy or light. It is not uncommon for vaginal bleeding to result at the time of implantation when the fertilized egg nestles into the wall of the uterus, approximately fourteen days after conception. Since that is also the time that most women expect their period, it is easy to confuse the two.

## Medical Care

Most obstetricians would like to see a future mother even before she attempts to conceive. This allows for a thorough review of her medical history so that problems can be identified and corrected early. Since most teen pregnancies are unintended and come as something of a surprise, a teenager should see a doctor as soon as she suspects pregnancy.

How does a doctor decide on a due date? As a rule a baby is due forty weeks after the first day of the last menstrual period. Forty weeks is actually nine months and seven days. That is why the due date is calculated by subtracting three months from the first day of the last menstrual period and then adding seven days. Thus, if the end of the last period were November 24, three months earlier would be August 24. Then if seven days were added, the due date would be calculated to be August 31.

A baby is considered full term up to two weeks before and after the due date. Less than 10 percent of babies are actually born on their due date. It is usually a good idea to keep a written record of menstrual bleeding, since one never knows when their current period will become their "last" menstrual period. After the first visit to the doctor, those who wish to carry the pregnancy to term are asked to come back for brief checkups once a month for the first six months, twice a month for the seventh and eighth month and then every week until the baby is born. During these visits the blood pressure, weight, baby's heartbeat, and abdominal growth are checked. A sample of urine is also tested for excessive protein or sugar.

Obstetricians generally recommend that the average pregnant woman gain twenty-five to thirty pounds during the course of the pregnancy. This average assumes that the patient is not significantly overweight or underweight at the time of conception. A pregnant woman should not eat for two; if she does, she will gain too much weight. Most women do well if they increase their diet by only 300 calories per day. It is also important to eat a variety of healthful foods such as poultry, meat, vegetables, dairy products, and fruit. Not included on this list are those foods that teenagers are notorious for eating: sweets, french fries, potato chips, and other related junk foods.

Expectant mothers should avoid substances, such as alcohol and other drugs. Tobacco products, alcohol, and illegal drugs are all known to damage a baby in the womb. Specifically, smoking results in premature and underweight babies. Alcohol use can causes mental retardation and abnormalities in a baby's appearance. The use of alcohol by mothers is the largest single correctable cause of mental retardation in the United States. The use of illegal drugs by pregnant women can lead to birth defects, stunted growth, or even the death of the unborn baby.

## How the Baby Grows

By about seven weeks after the last menstrual period a baby has a beating heart big enough to be seen in an ultrasound examination. At the beginning of the fourth month he or she has bones in arms and legs. Four weeks, later it is possible to tell the sex of a baby by ultrasound. Halfway through the pregnancy, at twenty weeks, a baby weighs almost a pound and has fingers and toes.

At twenty-four weeks a baby weighs an average of one and one-half pounds. Despite their development at this time, very few babies could survive outside the womb. As the weeks progress, more and more could live if born prematurely. At twenty-eight weeks many babies can survive, although they weigh only two pounds. When a baby weighs over three pounds it has both toenails and fingernails.

A woman will not lose all the weight she gained during pregnancy upon giving birth. Of the twenty-five to thirty pounds that most expectant mothers gain, a baby typically weighs seven to eight pounds. The placenta to which the umbilical cord is attached weighs about two pounds, as does the amniotic fluid that surrounds the baby. Both the womb and the breasts also are increased in size by two pounds each. Extra bodily fluid and blood add roughly six pounds to her weight. If you ate a well-balance and healthy diet during your pregnancy, you shouldn't have any trouble losing the weight after pregnancy.

## Pregnancy in the Teen Years

As noted in the introduction, the United States has one of the highest teenage pregnancy rates among developed countries. Almost 40 percent of females in the United States become pregnant by the age of nineteen. Despite the wide availability of contraceptive materials, an increasing number of teens become pregnant. Many people look upon this as a failure of schools and parents to teach teens how to make wise choices and to give them information needed to help them make these choices.

# PART II
# CONTRACEPTION

# Is It Safe
# and Effective?

Contraceptive choice is a highly personal matter that needs to be agreed upon by both partners. There are a variety of effective methods of birth control, but there is no single right choice for everybody.

Since there are so many types of birth control available today, it is best to speak with a doctor and ask questions. Tell your doctor what you want from a birth control method. Ask questions about anything you're unsure of. Your doctor will then give you some recommendations, but the final decision will be yours.

## Contraceptive Safety

Contraceptive methods rarely impair the user's health. The complication rate of all of them is so low that it has to be measured in terms of one in ten thousand to one in one hundred thousand users. The specific health risks of each contraceptive method are discussed in later chapters.

All forms of contraception discussed in this book are safer than carrying a pregnancy to term. More precisely, the risks of becoming ill or dying among women who have sex are higher when no birth control method is used because birth control, such as a condom, can reduce the risk of contracting STDs.

30

Finally, some contraceptives have benefits that can be a factor in the decision to use them. For example, the condom may provide some protection against the spread of sexually transmitted disease. The birth control pill can greatly reduce menstrual blood loss or cramps and is even thought to have some positive benefit in reducing the rate of death related to some forms of cancer. In fact, doctors often prescribe the pill even to those who are not sexually active just to reduce menstrual cramps or assure regular periods in women who do not have predictable cycles.

## Contraceptive Effectiveness

Data that asses a method's effectiveness are in some ways just as complicated as data on contraceptive safety. What are the chances that a couple who has sex twice a week for a year will conceive if they do not use contraception? Eighty to 90 percent of such couples will conceive within the year. About 20 percent of teenage girls conceive within the first month of losing their virginity, and half become pregnant within the first six months of sexual activity. Clearly, the chances are good for pregnancy if contraception is not used.

The effectiveness of a birth control method can be stated either as the percentage of women who conceive during one year despite its use or the percentage of women who do not conceive while using the method. For example, with the use of a given method, 85 percent of the women using it do not conceive in one year versus the 15 percent who do become pregnant.

A key factor in estimating the success rate of any method is the motivation of users. Birth control is only effective if it is used correctly according to instructions. A diaphragm in a drawer or a birth control pill in a medicine cabinet does not protect against pregnancy. As a result, birth control effectiveness is often described as a best rate and a typical rate.

In the table showing the effectiveness of various contraceptive methods, the percentages refer to those women who will become pregnant in a year—the smaller the number, the better the method. Each method is described in detail in the following chapters. Methods marked with an asterisk are either not widely available in the United States or are not appropriate for teens; they have been included to give a broader view of contraceptive effectiveness. Two asterisks indicate that, although the method is better than nothing, it should not be used as the chief method of birth control. The best methods are at the top of the table; the least effective ones at the bottom.

The pill may often be the contraceptive of choice for young women who do not have more than one sexual partner in a year, but a condom should always be used. If you or he has had other sexual partners, both of you may have contracted an STD from your previous partners. Also there are young people who believed they were in monogamous relationship were unwittingly exposed to STDs because their partners slept with other people during the relationship.

Withdrawal or douching methods over an extended period of time will almost surely become pregnant.

## Chances of Pregnancy (% in One Year of Use)

| Method | Best Rate | Typical Rate |
|---|---|---|
| Total abstinence | 0.0 | 0.0 |
| Norplant | 0.1 | 0.1 |
| Injectable progestin | 0.25 | 0.25 |
| Combined birth control pill | 0.5 | 2 |
| Progestin-only pill | 1 | 2.5 |
| IUD | 1.5 | 5 |
| Condom | 2 | 10 |
| Cervical cap* | 2 | 13 |
| Diaphragm (with spermicide) | 2 | 19 |
| Foams, creams, jellies, and vaginal suppositories | 3–5 | 18 |
| Withdrawal** | 16 | 23 |
| Periodic abstinence | 2–20 | 24 |
| Douche** | — | 40 |
| No method | 90 | 90 |

(Adapted with permission from Contraceptive Technology 1986–1987, pg. 102, Irvington Publishers, Inc., 740 Broadway, New York, NY 10003.)

* Not widely available or not often recommended for teens

** Very poor method of birth control

Many teens believe that if they have not conceived after a few episodes or even months of unprotected intercourse, they will not conceive in the future. There is overwhelming evidence that indicates this idea is false.

# Abstinence and
# Periodic Abstinence

This chapter examines two extremes of contraception: total abstinence and periodic abstinence. Total abstinence is the single most effective method of birth control, whereas periodic abstinence is among the least effective methods. Two other widely used but poor methods of contraception, withdrawal and douching, are also discussed.

## Total Abstinence

Simply stated, total abstinence means no sex. Unfortunately, even this idea is not as simple as it sounds. Does no sex mean no kissing or hugging? What about petting?

Whenever the penis releases sperm, there is a chance of pregnancy if any of the semen gets into or near (within a few inches) the vagina. If a man ejaculates on a woman's inner thigh, a pregnancy can occur if the sperm are carried into the vaginal opening. Even fingers can carry sperm into the vagina.

I will never forget the time I delivered the baby of a teenage virgin. The patient could not have intercourse because she had a sexual problem called vaginismus, in which her vaginal muscles involuntarily contracted whenever she attempted intercourse. Even so, her boyfriend ejaculated outside her vagina and, somehow, she conceived.

In any case, my definition of total abstinence is a narrow one. For me, no sex means never having the penis inside the vagina or in contact with the vagina, and there should be no genital to mouth contact. With this rule, total abstinence should be close to perfect in preventing pregnancy.

Total abstinence has another benefit. Without genital-to-genital contact or genital-to-mouth contact, the spread of a variety of diseases is almost impossible. As an obstetrician-gynecologist, I have seen young women who have contracted both herpes and genital warts from only one episode of intercourse. But if the penis never touches the vagina or the mouth, these diseases are not transmitted.

Is there any danger in total abstinence? Absolutely not. The myths about pent-up sexual energy causing bodily damage are false. People do not go blind or grow hair on the palms of their hands if they do not have sex or if their only sexual outlet is through masturbation or self-stimulation. Males will not get acne or suffer any harm. It is no more difficult for a young man to stop sexual activity before it leads to sexual intercourse than it is for a young woman.

Just because many teens are having sex does not mean that it is the right thing to do or a good idea. Saying no to sex is the best way to be assured of saying no to disease and unwanted pregnancy.

**Periodic Abstinence**
This method is actually a group of methods based on avoiding sex during a woman's fertile time. Periodic abstinence is also known as the "rhythm method" and as "natural family planning." It is a complicated technique that does not work

very well under the best of circumstances. Because of the difficulty in learning it and its high failure rate, periodic abstinence is a bad method for teens. It is the only method approved by the Catholic Church for married couples. The church is emphatically against premarital sex, with or without contraception.

Periodic abstinence relies on some guessing about when a woman is ovulating or releasing her egg, since she can conceive if she has sex up to six days before ovulation and perhaps one or two days afterward. In other words, women can get pregnant during only seven to eight days of the month. Periodic abstinence requires that she not have sex during the six days before ovulation and one to two days afterward. The problem is that it is very difficult to predict when a woman will ovulate. As a result, the longer a couple abstains in mid-cycle, the better the method will work. The method requires avoidance of sex when most couples might normally have sex—between menstrual periods.

Four basic methods can be used to make an educated guess as to when a woman will ovulate: calendar, basal body temperature, cervical mucus, and ovulation detection kits. The best results are obtained if more than one method is used. Speak with a doctor if you want more information about these methods.

## Method Summary
Periodic abstinence has serious drawbacks for teens. First, many young women do not have established menstrual cycles, making ovulation prediction difficult. Second, the methods are complicated and, except for ovulation detection kits, need months of practice before sex takes place.

Ovulation prediction does not work in a variety of circumstances. As mentioned above, teens in their first few years of menstruation often ovulate at unpredictable intervals. Periods should be regular for a full year before this method is tried. It also does not work for nursing mothers or women who have stopped the birth control pill within the past three months.

## Methods that Do Not Work Very Well

Two favorite, but ineffective birth control methods of teens, withdrawal and douching, should be reviewed. Some teens douche after intercourse in the unfounded hope that it will prevent pregnancy.

An even more popular method of birth control is withdrawal. Simply stated, the man removes his penis from the vagina just before his orgasm. While this method is somewhat better than no protection at all, it has several drawbacks. First, most men leak a little bit of sperm prior to ejaculation. The sperm leaked out is enough to impregnate a woman. The biggest drawback, however, is that most men cannot reliably remove the penis from the vagina just before orgasm. Some cannot tell in advance when they are going to climax, and others simply do not have the willpower or do not want to stop sex at the height of their pleasure.

# Oral Contraception

The birth control pill is by far the most effective form of reversible contraception. It is the only method that is reliable, is readily available, and does not require genital touching before and after sex. Despite its advantages, many misconceptions about the pill's safety discourage some teens who should be using it.

## History

The history of the pill is one of innovation and cost reduction. A chemist, Russell Marker, was able to achieve a remarkable reduction in the cost of producing the hormone progesterone. This enabled biologists to have ready access to the hormone for experimentation. Such work ultimately led to the development of a synthetic compound similar to progesterone that could be taken orally.

Progesterone is one of the key female hormones and is produced by the ovary in the second half of the menstrual cycle. At the time of Russell Marker's early hormone research, the ovaries from 2,500 slaughtered pigs were required to produce a fraction of an ounce of progesterone.

Marker's quest to lower the cost of progesterone took him to Mexico where he developed a cheap method of producing the hormone from the Mexican yam. As a result of Marker's efforts, the price of progesterone fell overnight from $200 a gram to $2. This development spurred interest in a more efficient production of a variety of hormones and the creation of new ones. Ultimately, scientists developed the oral contraceptive pill in the early 1950s.

## How It Works

The pill consists of two synthetic hormones that fool the body into thinking it is pregnant. As a result, the ovaries halt the release of an egg as they do when a woman is truly pregnant. This explanation is somewhat oversimplified because the pill acts to prevent pregnancy by other means as well.

In addition to preventing ovulation, the pill also causes changes in the cervical mucus that reduce the number of sperm able to enter the uterus. It may also have an effect on the tubes that interferes with the movement of sperm and egg. Whatever the case, its most important action is the prevention of ovulation.

## How to Take the Pill

There are two types of pills: the twenty-one-day pill and the twenty-eight-day pill. They cost exactly the same and are available in different brands and doses. The twenty-eight-day pill has seven extra inactive pills that are supposed to be reminders to take the pill every day. The twenty-one-day pill is taken for twenty-one days in a row but skips the next seven days. A light menstrual period will occur in the fourth week with either the twenty-one- or twenty-eight-day pill. Most women (teens included) prefer the twenty-one-day package because they do not want to bother with taking the seven placebo pills.

Other contraceptive methods should also be used in the first month of pill use since the pill does not always prevent ovulation in the first cycle. Some doctors may suggest using another method for only the first two weeks.

The pill should be kept in a place that helps you to remember to take it and close to other items used in the daily routine, such as toothpaste. It is best to take the pill at about the same time each day.

Starting the first pack is the most confusing part of taking the pill. There are three common ways to do this, depending on the type of pill chosen and the doctor's advice. All of the pills can be started in any one of these ways; sometimes the labeling and packaging make one set of directions easier to follow than another.

## Sunday Start

This is the method that I recommend for my patients, chiefly because many brands come labeled for starting use on a Sunday. The pill is to be started on the first Sunday after the beginning of the menstrual period (not after it ends). It should be taken on that Sunday whether or not the menstrual period has ended.

| *First Day of Vaginal Bleeding* | *Start Pill on Sunday* |
|---|---|
| Monday | Six days later |
| Tuesday | Five days later |

41

| Wednesday | Four days later |
| Thursday | Three days later |
| Friday | Two days later |
| Saturday | The next day |
| Sunday | That same day |

With the Sunday start method, the pill should never be started more than six days after the first day of the period.

**Fifth-day Start**
Simply start the pill on the fifth day of the cycle (day one is the first day of your period).

**First-day Start**
Start the pill on the first day of vaginal bleeding. Whatever method is used, all subsequent packs should be started on the same day as the first pack and exactly twenty-eight days later—whether or not a period has started or ended. In general, your period will occur in the fourth week of each cycle.

The above instructions apply only when first starting the pill. Once the very first pill is taken, the rest have to be taken correctly to prevent conception and the instructions no longer depend on the woman's bleeding pattern. This is especially important in view of the fact that irregular bleeding is quite common in the first few months on the pill. Bleeding is supposed to occur in the fourth week (the off week for those on the twenty-one-day pill and the last week for those on the twenty-eight-day pill). Women frequently experience bleeding before this time and occasionally they won't get their period at all. Regardless of the bleeding pattern, the pill must continue to be taken on a rigid schedule. Skipping pills or stopping in midcycle will cause unpredictable bleeding to continue. Once on the pill, a new package must be started on the same day four weeks later regardless of the bleeding pattern.

## Forgetting the Pill

The pill does not prevent pregnancy if it is not taken correctly. It is only human to forget to take a pill once in a while, but such forgetting should not be taken lightly. This error slightly reduces the protection of the pill for that cycle, but if the directions below are followed the risk is small.

One pill forgotten—Take two pills the next day as soon as you remember, and then resume your daily schedule.

Two pills forgotten—Some doctors suggest that you take two pills as soon as you remember and then two pills again the next day. They may or may not recommend that another method of contraception be used for the rest of the cycle.

I recommend that the pill be stopped for that cycle and that the partially used pack be thrown away. Patients should use other contraception, such as the condom, and start the pill all over again with the next menstrual cycle. The pill just does not work very well if it is not taken every day in accordance with instructions.

## Stopping the Pill

Stopping the pill is quite easy. Simply do not start the next pack. There is actually no harm in stopping in the middle of a cycle, but irregular bleeding is more likely to occur. Once the pill is stopped, the first few periods may be infrequent and irregular.

## Side Effects

As a rule, most side effects of the pill, which are noted below, resolve within three months of use. If they do not, a different pill can often be substituted with good results.

### Weight Gain
This effect is often temporary. It is a problem in only a minority of patients.

### Nausea
Some women experience nausea shortly after starting the pill. This problem usually disappears by the third month. Taking the pill on a full stomach or just before bedtime can help. If nausea persists, your doctor may prescribe a different brand.

### Depression
This side effect is not very common. It is typically the kind of depression that lasts through several cycles and is more than just moodiness or irritability. Although some women may experience moodiness on the pill, other causes, often unknowable are usually accountable for mood swings in pill users.

However, if your depression doesn't seem to be going away, you should see a doctor about the problem.

## Irregular Bleeding

The most common problems for those just starting the pill are that bleeding can occur in midcycle or the menses may not happen at all. In general, all birth control pills tend to reduce cramping and bleeding during menstruation. They do this so well that it is a major benefit of the pill and sometimes is the chief reason that doctors prescribe it for some women. However, the same mechanism of the pill that reduces period discomfort can also cause unpredictable bleeding.

The mixture of hormones in the pill causes the uterine lining to thin out somewhat. This is why most people have less menstrual bleeding on the pill. However, this same mechanism can thin the uterine lining so much that one of two things happens: either the uterine lining can be so thin that there is simply nothing to shed at the end of the cycle, or the fragile blood vessels lining the uterine cavity can break in midcycle. Thus two opposite problems—no period and unpredictable bleeding—can have the same cause. Neither problem is a threat to health nor do they suggest that the pill is not working. Irregular bleeding is a common problem in a minority of women using a particular brand.

If you experience two cycles in a row of midcycle bleeding on the pill and are bothered by it, ask your doctor to prescribe a different brand.

A complete absence of menstrual periods is a somewhat different problem. Although a missed period is not dangerous, it can also be one of the first signs of pregnancy. If you do not have a period following each cycle of pill use, you should consult your doctor after doing a home pregnancy test. If you're not pregnant and and taking the pill results in no periods, be assured that the circumstance is not dangerous. Your doctor can start you on a different brand of pills that will not affect your periods.

## Health Benefits

In addition to its principal function of preventing pregnancy, the pill has several health benefits. Some of these benefits are so significant that the pill may occasionally be prescribed for women who do not need contraception.

### Reduction of Menstrual Cramps
As mentioned previously, the pill greatly reduces painful cramping in those who have difficult periods.

### Reduction of Menstrual Flow
It also reduces menstrual bleeding by an average of one third. As a result, anemia is less common among pill users.

### Protection against PID (Pelvic Inflammatory Disease)
Although the pill does not prevent the spread of sexually transmitted disease, it seems to reduce the chance of contracting a serious pelvic infection from gonorrhea.

### Prevention of Ovarian Cysts
As mentioned earlier, it is normal and necessary to have cysts on the ovary when ovulating. Occasionally, one of these cysts may grow larger than two and one-half inches or so. At this point, the doctor cannot be sure if it is a normal

cyst or an abnormal growth on the ovary. Since the pill prevents ovulation and cyst formation, it is sometimes given to women who have a large cyst. If the cyst remains while the patient is on the pill, it is more likely to be an abnormal growth that requires removal. If it goes away, nothing further is required, and the pill can be stopped if it is not needed for contraception.

### Protection against Cancer
Many women mistakenly think that the pill causes cancer, whereas the reverse is true. The pill almost certainly provides protection against uterine and ovarian cancer.

### Elimination of Midcycle Pain
As described in chapter 6 about periodic abstinence, some women experience midcycle pain when the egg is released from the ovary. Since the pill blocks ovulation, it completely eliminates this type of monthly pain.

### Protection against Arthritis
Although not usually a concern for teenagers, the pain of rheumatoid arthritis seems to be reduced or prevented when the pill is used.

## Health Risks

Using the pill for one year is at least twice as safe as carrying a pregnancy to term. The most important (but rare) danger of the pill is the increased tendency of a few users to develop blood clots, which can lead to a heart attack and a stroke. The pill can also cause high blood pressure, although this problem is not common with lower-dose pills. The elevated blood pressure returns to normal when the pill is stopped. There may also be a slight increase in the frequency of gallbladder disease, although this too is rare. In general, the risk of health problems is so small that it should not be a major consideration in use of this method.

Smoking increases the dangers of stroke among women who are on the pill, although the danger is not usually enough to prevent doctors from prescribing it. An important fact to keep in mind is that smokers are more likely to have strokes and heart attacks whether or not they are on the pill. In fact, smoking is a very serious roadblock to good health.

## Obtaining the Pill

The pill must be prescribed by a physician. Before prescribing it, your doctor will usually require a complete physical examination. I prescribe the pill if a woman does not have high blood pressure and has a normal exam which virtually all of our patients do. I see patients again three months after they start the pill, a pelvic exam is not done the second time. If they are not having any problems on the pill and have normal blood pressure, give them a prescription for nine months and then examine them once a year. Smokers on the pill should see their doctors every six months. Some doctors will see nonsmokers who are on the pill every six months. Differences between physicians' practices with regard to women on the pill often reflect the fact that a the physicians in question may be treating different patient populations.

The cost of the pill runs about $25 per month—up to $300 per year. Although a yearly exam by the physician costs between $80 and $150, any sexually active woman should have a checkup at least once a year. Some clinics and doctors have access to discounted pills and, occasionally, will give sample packs to teens. In most states, doctors do not need parental permission to prescribe the pill, and they are usually careful to keep patient and medication information confidential—particularly from parents if the patient so desires. If you are worried about confidentiality or your parents finding out, simply call a doctor's office anonymously and ask about the policy regarding the prescribing of pills for teenagers.

## Generic Birth Control Pills

I strongly recommend generic birth control pills to my patients, as do many other physicians. These typically cost is $12 to $15 per month, which may mean a savings of greater than 50 percent over the brand names. The makers of brand-name pills talk vaguely of quality issues, but there is no evidence that generic pills are any less safe or effective than brand-name pills, nor have I seen any evidence in my practice to make me think that there is any measurable difference.

When the patent expires on any drug, competitors can obtain the publicly available ingredients and manufacture the medication on their own. This happens with all successful pharmaceutical products, including heart medication and antibiotics. Generic birth control pills can save you $100 or more per year if you choose to take them. Simply remind your doctor that price is very important to you, and he or she will review your prescription options.

# Norplant
# Contraception

The Norplant system of contraception consists of six silastic tubes placed just under the skin on the underside of one arm. Norplant provides five years of pregnancy protection and is completely reversible.

## How Does It Work?

Norplant prevents pregnancy in much the same way as the birth control pill. It prevents the woman from ovulating, and it causes the mucus secreted by the cervix to thicken somewhat, thereby making it more difficult for sperm to swim up the reproductive tract. Birth control pills contain both synthetic estrogen and progesterone, whereas Norplant contains only one type of progesterone. As a result, some women who have side effects with the birth control pill may not experience those problems with Norplant.

## Is It Safe and Effective?

Norplant is both extremely safe and effective. It is not known or suspected to increase the risk of any type of cancer. It has no harmful effect on health and does not affect fertility. Within months of removal, women rapidly experience a rapid return to their pre-Norplant level of fertility. If they had irregular periods prior to using Norplant, they are likely to have irregular periods after it is removed.

While pregnancy does occur in women using Norplant, it is so uncommon that pregnancy rates over five years of Norplant use are less than those for women who have been sterilized by tubal ligation. Because there is nothing to remember, it is much more effective than even the birth control pill. Fewer than one patient in every hundred conceives over five years of use.

If you experience regular periods on Norplant and they suddenly stop, you should check for pregnancy. Also, when Norplant is first placed and you have no period, it might not be a bad idea to do a home pregnancy test. Again, pregnancy is very unlikely once Norplant is in place.

## Advantages

- ↝ Extremely effective

- ↝ Completely reversible

- ↝ Nothing to remember

- ↝ No estrogen

## Disadvantages

- ↝ Small surgical procedure required to insert and remove.

51

⮑ High likelihood of menstrual irregularities. Bleeding irregularities with Norplant include any combination of the following patterns: no periods or bleeding at all, long menstrual periods, and bleeding between menstrual periods.

Generally, bleeding irregularity diminishes by the end of one year of use, and total blood loss per year is actually reduced in those using Norplant. However, the potential for unpredictable bleeding may be worrisome. This side effect is the biggest disadvantage in using Norplant. Also, this bleeding is not easily treatable short of removing Norplant. Even with this potential problem, however, 80 percent of women who begin Norplant continue with it after one year.

## Risks

The risks of using Norplant are small. Serious complications are extremely rare. Relatively minor dangers include the potential for infection at the insertion site, expulsion of one or more of the capsules, or difficulty in subsequent removal. If removal of all the implants proves difficult at the time you wish to discontinue Norplant, a second removal attempt may be necessary four weeks later. Keep in mind that difficulties in removing the implants may be messy and can leave scars.

## Side Effects

Side effects (other than bleeding irregularities) that are

possible but uncommon include pain or itching at the insertion site, headache, nervousness, dizziness, skin irritation, acne, appetite change, breast tenderness, weight gain, and hair growth or loss. Should any of these side effects occur, they will often resolve themselves after a few months of use and are totally reversible after Norplant's removal.

## Insertion Procedure

Norplant needs to be inserted within seven days of the beginning of a menstrual period. It costs between $500 and $800 to insert and must be obtained through a doctor. The removal procedure has an additional cost, generally between $100 and $300. While gynecologists are the only doctors who can perform the procedure, not all gynecologists do it. Make sure your doctor is able to do it.

Norplant can be inserted in the doctor's office. Frequently, doctors require two visits. On the first you are examined and counseled. If you decide that you still want Norplant, you may return for the insertion procedure at the appropriate time.

The procedure itself takes ten to fifteen minutes. Injection of an anesthetic beneath the skin on the underside of your arm can be somewhat uncomfortable—similar to a blood draw. The remainder of the procedure probably will not bother you since you will be numb at the insertion site. The doctor makes a small skin incision (about a quarter of an inch long). Six silastic tubes are then pushed through a hollow tube placed just under the skin and deposited there.

After the procedure, one or two small Band-aids are placed over the insertion site and covered with gauze. Leave the gauze in place for twenty-four hours, after which time you may remove it. Keep your arm dry during this time period. After three days, you may remove the tapes. Call your doctor if you have redness, pain, or pus oozing from the insertion site.

## Removal Procedure

Removal is similar to insertion. You are given an injection of anesthetic and a small incision is made. Small instruments are then used to remove each of the silastic tubes. A fresh set of Norplant capsules may be inserted at the same time if you wish. The removal procedure has an additional cost, but many doctors have yet to establish a standard price. It is likely to be between $100 and $300. With both the insertion and removal procedures included, Norplant is still cheaper than using brand-name birth control pills for five years.

# Other Types of Hormonal Contraception

Aside from the standard birth control pill, hormones can be used in several other ways to prevent pregnancy. These include the progestin-only pill, hormone injections (Depo-Provera), and the morning-after pill. Each of these methods has disadvantages when compared to the birth control pill. None are commonly prescribed for teens, but they may be used in special circumstances.

## The Progestin-Only Pill

Rather than the standard two synthetic hormones that are used in birth control pills, this pill has only a very small dose of one of the hormones, a synthetic progestin. It is slightly less effective than the usual birth control pill and may not prevent ovulation as effectively. The reason this pill has not become very popular is because many people have long-lasting irregular bleeding that can be quite disruptive. It is used for some women who develop high blood pressure or other side effects while on the standard combination pill.

## Depo-Provera

Depo-Provera is a long-acting hormone that is administered

by injection every three months. Depo-Provera works by blocking ovulation. This method has several drawbacks, however. First, while it works for only three months, it may actually impair fertility for up to a year—not usually a big disadvantage for teens. Irregular bleeding may also be a problem, although the most common side effect is the lack of menstrual periods altogether. However, many women consider this to be a benefit, not a disadvantage. Finally, depression may be somewhat more common (though still rare) with this drug than with regular birth control pills. If it occurs, the depression tends to last as long as the Depo-Provera is taken.

## The Morning-After Pill

This is one method that some teens may have occasion to need. Most commonly prescribed following a rape, some gynecologists also dispense it in the case of an accident. It is meant only for one-time protection after the fact and cannot be used for regular contraception.

With this method, two hormone pills are taken at once and then repeated in twelve hours. It has to be taken within forty-eight hours of intercourse. Many people are nauseated by this medication, so gynecologists may also prescribe an antinausea medication.

Should pregnancy result in spite of the use of this drug, there is significant concern about birth defects, since the embryo would have been exposed to a large amount of hormone. Many doctors may recommend abortion if pregnancy results despite the use of the morning-after pill.

## Summary

The standard birth control pill is more effective than the progestin-only pill, more reversible than hormone injections, and safer than the morning-after pill. Teens are not given the medications discussed in this chapter except in unusual circumstances.

# The IUD

The letters IUD stand for Intrauterine Device (within the uterus). It is rarely the method of choice for teenagers. A bit of history on the IUD illustrates its disadvantages for teenagers.

## History

The first IUD as we have come to know it in the twentieth century was introduced in 1909 and was made of silkworm gut. A German doctor developed the so-called Grafenberg ring, which became popular in Germany in the 1930s. At the same time an IUD was being used in Japan. By the 1960s American manufacturers began producing various plastic devices in large quantities. In the late 1970s copper was added to some of the plastic IUDs to make them more effective.

Today, the IUD is manufactured under the brand name Paragard. This is a T-shaped piece of plastic surrounded by thin copper wire that increases its effectiveness.

While many doctors are appropriately reluctant to give the IUD to teens, the contraceptive device does have its role. The IUD is close to a perfect form of contraception for married women who have completed their families.

## How It Works

No one is sure why the IUD protects against pregnancy. Some suspect it may prevent the fertilized egg from implanting and growing on the wall of the uterus. It may also block the passage of sperm into the fallopian tubes. Adding copper to an IUD seems to increase its effectiveness slightly, although no one understands why. Some IUDs also have hormones added to them. Thus far, the hormones last only from twelve to eighteen months, and these IUDs have to be replaced more frequently than the copper IUDs.

Whatever IUD is used, the method is highly effective, particularly since there is nothing to be remembered before having sex. Theoretically, the IUD should be 99 percent effective, but because it can be expelled from the uterus without the woman's knowledge, the true effectiveness is roughly 97 percent—better than the condom but not quite as good as the pill.

## How to Use It

Available only from a doctor, the IUD takes only five minutes to insert and is not very uncomfortable. Plain plastic IUDs can be worn for years at a time. The somewhat more effective copper IUDs must be replaced every ten years because the copper is absorbed by the body and disappears over time. Medicated IUDs, such as those with hormones added, need to be replaced every year or so. The IUD is made with a string attached to its tail. A string passes through the cervix into the vagina, where it can be seen or felt. This string needs to be checked at the end of each menstrual period. If it cannot be detected, a physician should be notified. It is possible for the uterus to reject the IUD without a woman's knowledge. This usually happens during the cramping of the menstrual period. If the IUD is expelled, a woman is no longer protected. Many people have conceived because they did not realize that their IUD had been expelled. Teens who have never given birth before, have a slightly higher chance of their body expelling the IUD.

In general, women who have had children have less trouble with the IUD than those who have not, simply because the uterus has been slightly enlarged through the course of childbearing.

An IUD is easiest to insert and remove during the first few days of a menstrual period. The cervical canal dilates slightly at this time, and menstruation indicates that the woman is not pregnant. Most people do not require any pain medicine or anesthetic before the insertion. Removing the IUD is even easier and faster.

An IUD itself costs $230, and its insertion by a physician costs approximately $150. There is a separate charge of about $150 to remove it. However, since the IUD can be worn for up to ten years, its cost per year, including insertion and removal, is roughly $50. This is comparable to one year's expenditure on condoms and is much cheaper than a twelve-month supply of the pill.

## Safety

It is important to realize that the use of all contraceptive methods, including the IUD, are safer over the course of a year than being pregnant. Even so, the IUD does have specific risks and health disadvantages.

Although mishaps during IUD insertion are quite rare (once every 2,000 times or so), the IUD can also cause difficulties once it is in the uterus. As a rule, menstrual periods are heavier with this method of contraception. Specifically, women tend to bleed more and have greater cramping. Medication, such as ibuprofen, can decrease menstrual discomfort, but some women experience a notable change for the worse in their menses and will have the IUD removed.

The major controversy over the IUD is the risk of a serious pelvic infection called pelvic inflammatory disease (PID). Simply stated, PID is a complication of a bacterial infection that is usually caused by gonorrhea or chlamydia. It can cause fever, pelvic pain, and subsequent damage to the fallopian tubes leading to infertility. It seems that this infection occurs more frequently in women wearing an IUD, although it is not clear why. One theory is that the string leading from the sterile uterus into the vagina may make it easier for infection to enter the womb.

For those wearing an IUD, two important points should be remembered in considering the risk of PID. First, the overall incidence of PID in users of recently marketed IUDs is rather low—roughly 2.5 per 1,000 women in one year of use (in comparison with 1 per 1,000 among diaphragm users). Second, and more important, pelvic inflammatory disease is not exclusive to IUD users. It is a sexually transmitted disease. Although the IUD can increase the complication rate of bacterial infections, it does not increase the odds that an individual will contract gonorrhea. Rather, odds are strongly influenced by the number of sexual partners a woman has over a given period of time. As a result,

61

when IUDs became more readily available, many physicians gave them only to married women and had completed their family.

## What if Pregnancy Occurs?

Roughly one in twenty women conceives during one year of IUD use. What happens to the woman, the IUD, and the pregnancy? If the IUD is not removed, about half of these women will miscarry. Those who do not miscarry generally carry the baby to full term without difficulties. Contrary to popular belief, if the pregnancy is not lost in the first twelve weeks, the IUD does not injure the developing baby or cause birth defects. The baby simply grows away from the IUD.

However, if the IUD is removed in the first trimester, the chances of a successful pregnancy are somewhat higher than if it is left in place. For this reason, if a woman wants to keep the pregnancy the IUD is removed as soon as possible.

Another controversy surrounding the IUD is its effect on ectopic pregnancies. In such pregnancies, the fertilized egg grows outside the womb, usually within the fallopian tube. These pregnancies can never survive because the only place that a fetus can get proper nourishment is within the uterus. Unfortunately, IUDs also pose a serious threat to the mother since they can continue to grow until the fallopian tube breaks open. That is not only very painful but is usually associated with life-threatening internal bleeding. This complication requires emergency surgery to repair any damage.

In any event, some people mistakenly believe that wearing an IUD increases the risk of having an ectopic pregnancy. This is not the case, although it is true that those few women who do conceive while wearing an IUD are more likely to have a tubal pregnancy than women not using IUDs. This confusing situation occurs because the IUD is most effective in preventing pregnancies within the womb. As a result, though somewhat fewer ectopic pregnancies seem to occur, they compose a higher fraction of all pregnancies among IUD users than among nonusers. The bottom line is that the IUD is an effective contraceptive that does not increase the overall risk of ectopic pregnancy and may actually reduce it slightly.

Any woman who becomes pregnant with an IUD in place should see her doctor within a week of finding out about the pregnancy. A doctor can then give more accurate direction about what steps to take next.

## IUDs and Teens

Doctors are reluctant to place IUDs in teens for two reasons. As stated before, teens who have yet to bear children, have a slightly greater percentage of expelling the IUD. Second, since most teens may have just begun to be sexually active, relatively few will have long-term monogamous relationships. Teenagers have a high rate of contracting sexually transmitted diseases. Since IUDs can increase the complication rate from bacteria, such as gonorrhea and chlamydia, most doctors don't recommend IUDs to teenagers.

## Summary

The IUD is a highly effective form of contraception that requires no special preparation prior to intercourse. It can make periods much more uncomfortable for some women, and it may increase the risk of serious pelvic infection, particularly women with more than one sexual partner per year. The IUD has no other significant health risks and is often ideal for married women who have finished childbearing.

# The Condom

An effective method of birth control, the condom has virtually no ill effects on health. Among the many nicknames for the condom are "prophylactic," "rubber," and "safe." A number of condom brands are available, including Trojan and Ramses.

A condom is a rubber shield that fits over the erect penis. A condom prevents sperm from entering the vagina by forming a barrier around the penis. This is the only method of birth control that prevents an exchange of bodily fluids during sex. This is important because STDs are caused by this exchange of body fluids, a condom greatly reduces the chances of transmitting or contracting an STD.

Even if you use other forms of birth control, you should always use it in conjunction with condoms. Although other methods protect against pregnancy, they do not provide protection from STDs, such as AIDS.

## How to Use a Condom

A condom is very thin and stretchable, and it unrolls to the necessary length. Using a condom is straightforward, but many people are self-conscious about it. Although it may feel strange to use a condom the first few times, you will get use to it. Using contraceptives is part of being sexually active.

To use the condom correctly:

1. It should be placed on the man's penis as soon as he becomes aroused. This is important because sperm can leak out of the penis during foreplay before he has an orgasm.

2. Half an inch or so of extra rubber should extend beyond the tip of the penis. If the condom is placed too tightly over the head of the penis, it is more likely to break when sperm is ejected during orgasm.

3. As soon as the man climaxes, he should grasp the base of the condom while his penis is still erect and withdraw from the vagina. If he fails to do this, the condom could slip off and spill sperm into the vagina when his erection subsides.

4. A condom should never be reused, nor should it be flushed down the toilet.

## Effects on Health

Use of a condom has absolutely no side effects or risks. Sometimes, a man or a woman may be allergic to the latex in condoms. This becomes apparent with the development of a rash that may itch.

## Effectiveness and Cost

A condom is more effective in preventing pregnancy than both spermicides and periodic abstinence. It is probably

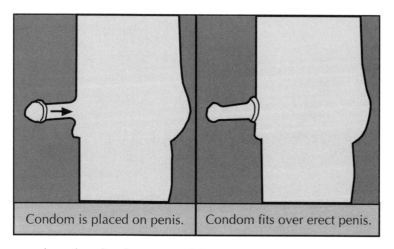

| Condom is placed on penis. | Condom fits over erect penis. |

equal to the diaphragm and less than the pill in terms of effectiveness. In general, of 100 couples who have intercourse on a regular basis for one year, only ten conceive (an effectiveness rate of 90 percent). If the same 100 couples are followed over five years, the pregnancy rate might be as high as 40 percent, depending on the motivation of the couple. If a condom is used without fail every time a couple has sex, the effectiveness can be even higher than 90 percent. The problem is that few people reliably use a condom whenever they have sex.

Pregnancy with condom use can also occur if the condom breaks open during ejaculation. However, this almost never happens if it is used correctly.

Condoms can be found in many places; they are widely available. They are sold in most grocery stores and drugstores. Many clinics and even some schools distribute condoms to teens.

Condoms come in a wide variety of colors and textures. The more expensive condoms are thinner but are not necessarily manufactured better or less likely to break. Some come lubricated, others with spermicide added. The effectiveness of condoms can be greatly increased by combining condoms with spermicide. They cost in the range of fifty cents to one dollar each, and are less when bought in quantity.

One important aspect of the condom is that, thus far, it is the only contraceptive that a man can use. Since condoms are widely available and very cheap, there should be no excuse for having unprotected intercourse.

# The Diaphragm and Cervical Cap

Although it was developed about 150 years ago, the diaphragm did not gain popularity until the 1900s. Before the advent of modern spermicides, the diaphragm was used with lubricants, such as butter and cocoa. However, use of spermicides, rather than foodstuffs, greatly improves the diaphragm's effectiveness.

## Where to Get It

Diaphragms come in different sizes and have to be obtained from a doctor. The diaphragm itself costs about $30 and can last for years. A special charge for fitting the diaphragm is about $50 in addition to the physician's fee for a regular checkup. A doctor or nurse teaches the patient how to insert the diaphragm. The patient can then practice several times in the doctor's office until she feels comfortable with the insertion process. It's very important that you know how to properly insert and remove a diaphragm correctly. If you do it wrong, it can result in pregnancy. The doctor may suggest that a patient return with the diaphragm in place so that its proper placement can be checked.

Typically the largest diaphragm that fits comfortably is prescribed. The diaphragm is designed to fit snugly in front of the cervix and is held up from behind by the back wall of the vagina. Its front support is the pubic bone.

The diaphragm size should be checked (a) after the birth of a baby, (b) after a twenty-pound weight gain or loss, and (c) after several episodes of intercourse if it was fitted prior to losing virginity. After each use, it should be washed with soap and water, rinsed thoroughly, and dried. It should be stored in its carrying case without powder; powder can cause the rubber to deteriorate. If the rubber becomes pockmarked or holes develop, it should be replaced immediately. The easiest method to check for holes is to hold the diaphragm against the light.

## How to Use It

One hour before having sex, the diaphragm should be placed inside the vagina. If it is inserted more than an hour prior to sex, additional spermicide should be placed in the vagina with an applicator (see chapter 13 on spermicide use). The diaphragm should be left in place for six to eight hours after sex. Additional spermicide should be used each time intercourse takes place. The diaphragm can be worn for twenty-four hours at a time without any difficulty. It should not interfere with urination or bowel movements, although rarely a very large bowel movement can push the diaphragm out.

## Insertion and Removal of the Diaphragm

1. Grasp the diaphragm, dome side down (as though it were a bowl). Put an ounce (one tablespoon) of

spermicidal cream or jelly into the bowl of the diaphragm and around the edges. The spermicide that you purchase should be labeled "for use with diaphragm"; this is because some spermicides can dissolve the rubber with repeated use.

2. Pinch the diaphragm in the middle and insert it by separating the lips of the vagina with the other hand. The diaphragm should be guided backward along the vaginal wall as far as it will go. It can be inserted from the following three positions:

➭ Lying flat on your back with knees bent and legs flexed outward

➭ Squatting

➭ Standing, with one leg raised (resting on a chair, side of the bathtub, etc.)

3. The position of the diaphragm should be checked at this point. It must be covering the cervix. The cervix has the same firmness as the front of the nose and has a small indentation in its center. It can be touched by reaching all they way back into the vagina.

The diaphragm should also be propped against the pubic bone in front. The back of this bone can be felt by placing a finger in the vagina and then reaching forward and upward. The bone extends over and to either side of the vagina. It can also be felt from the outside by pressing down over the pubic hair. The front part of the diaphragm should be resting against the back side of this bone.

4. Remove the diaphragm by placing a finger inside the vagina and reaching upward and forward to hook the rim with the finger. Then slide the diaphragm down and out.

## Safety and Effectiveness

Like the condom, diaphragm use carries no serious health risks. A few people can develop allergic reactions to either the spermicide or the latex in the diaphragm. These reactions may consist of itching or a rash but are rarely severe and usually resolve when the offending agent is no longer used.

Toxic shock syndrome (TSS), a rare bacterial illness, occurs in less than ten women among 100,000 users. Symptoms of TSS include a sunburn-like rash, fever, nausea, vomiting, and muscle aches. Should two or more of these symptoms occur at the same time, a physician should be consulted. The incidence of TSS is no more likely with the use of diaphragm than with tampon use. Those who have had toxic shock syndrome in the past should not use the diaphragm.

Used with spermicide, a diaphragm may provide some protection against the spread of sexually transmitted disease, although the extent of this protection is uncertain. One other small health benefit is that the diaphragm can be used to have sex during a menstrual period without it becoming too messy. When placed inside the vagina an hour or so before sex, the diaphragm will prevent menstrual blood from spilling out of the vagina. During a period the diaphragm should not be left in place for more than several hours. When properly fitted, the diaphragm should not interfere with the sensation or pleasure of sex.

The diaphragm has the same effectiveness as the condom—roughly 90 percent or higher if it is used without fail every time a couple has sex. When effectiveness is discussed, it is always assumed that spermicide is being used along with the diaphragm.

## The Cervical Cap

This contraceptive device has many similarities to the diaphragm. It is a rubber object inserted into the vagina and meant to fit the cervix snugly. Because it is smaller, the cervical cap can be worn for a longer period of time, but it is also more difficult to insert. It is not clear how long a cervical cap can be worn at one given time. Since it is more difficult to insert correctly and seems to offer no advantages over the diaphragm, the cap has not become very popular.

# Spermicides

Basically five forms of spermicides are available: vaginal suppositories, film, foam, jelly, and cream. Their effectiveness is very similar, and the form of spermicide chosen by the user is a matter of personal preference.

## How to Use Spermicides

Like the condom, spermicides are available without a prescription. They are usually displayed in the aisle containing feminine hygiene products.

Jellies or creams are inserted with the help of a vaginal applicator. The applicator is filled, inserted gently into the vagina as far as it will go, and the plunger is pressed. This forces the contents of the applicator into the vagina. The vaginal applicator that comes with a large tube of spermicide is meant to be used more than once. Packages of prefilled disposable applicators are also available.

To insert a suppository, it is simply removed from the wrapper and inserted deep into the vagina. A suppository should be given time to dissolve and disperse. It should be placed at least thirty minutes before intercourse.

A variation of the vaginal suppository is vaginal film. This is a thin, dry sheet of spermicide that is placed in the vagina up to thirty minutes prior to intercourse. The main difference between spermicide and jellies and film is that some people find the vaginal film to be less messy.

Before using foam, the container should be shaken well. The applicator should be placed as far into the vagina as possible. Foam provides protection as soon as it is administered, but its benefit lasts for only about thirty minutes. In general, foam tends to be the least messy, since it is composed largely of gas and spermicide. The gas escapes rapidly, leaving only spermicide behind.

## Safety and Effectiveness

When spermicide is used alone it is somewhat less effective than if it is combined with a diaphragm or condom. Its success rate runs in the 80 percent range. That is, 10 to 20 percent of women who use this method will become pregnant in the course of one year. Like other contraceptive methods, its effectiveness is highly dependent on how reliably it is used.

The use of these products carries no health risk, although some people may have genital irritation if they are allergic to any of the ingredients. Those who are allergic to one spermicide are often allergic to many others, since they largely contain the same ingredients.

Spermicides are detergents and act by disrupting the cell membrane of the sperm. This is key to understanding their protective effect against sexually transmitted diseases. At least in laboratories, spermicides have been shown to inactivate or destroy a variety of bacteria and viruses, including those that cause many of the sexually transmitted diseases. However, the condom still provides the best protection against STDs.

## The Condom and Spermicide

The combination of a condom and additional spermicide deserves special mention. These methods combined rival the effectiveness of the pill—pregnancy results only once in every 100 couples who reliably use the combination. Furthermore, the combination method has no health risks whatsoever other than a rare and mild allergic reaction. A significant benefit may be the ability of this combination to protect against STDs. The condom and spermicide each prevents the spread of STDs, such as AIDS, by different mechanisms. As a result, their use together represents the most effective method to protect against sexually transmitted diseases.

# Abortion

Abortion is not considered birth control. Birth control prevents a pregnancy from occurring. Abortion is the means to end a pregnancy. However, because some women are compelled to choose this option when they accidentally become pregnant so the issue of abortion needs to be addressed. Before abortion was legalized throughout the United States by the 1973 Supreme Court decision in *Roe vs. Wade*, obtaining an abortion was often a difficult and dangerous venture, which many women nonetheless undertook. While abortion remains a highly divisive issue, it is now a relatively inexpensive and safe procedure.

## Before the Abortion

The method of abortion chosen depends on the length of time that has elapsed since conception. Since most abortions are done in the first twelve weeks of pregnancy, this chapter focuses on those types of abortion. Procedures done much later in the pregnancy are more expensive and involved. They often require medication to induce labor and an overnight hospital stay. Abortions done early in the pregnancy take about fifteen minutes; a woman can go home the same day and go to work or school the next day.

Before an abortion can be done, the duration of the pregnancy has to be well defined. This is accomplished in several ways. First, a medical history is taken by a doctor to establish the date of the last menstrual period. Next, a physical exam is made to judge the size of the uterus. Often another pregnancy test is performed to further confirm the pregnancy. Occasionally, an ultrasound examination is required when there is a question about the duration of a pregnancy.

Depending upon where the abortion is being done, other tests are often performed, including blood tests for blood type and an anemia count. Sometimes tests for gonorrhea and chlamydia are done as well. At some point, most abortion centers provide a formal counseling session in which the procedure is discussed at length and the woman's desire to proceed is confirmed.

## Laminaria

Some abortion centers have the patient come in the day before the procedure for the initial medical evaluation and discussion. During this session, laminaria are sometimes inserted to make the abortion easier. Laminaria are thin sticks of sterilized, dry seaweed. While this sounds bizarre, laminaria swell when they absorb moisture. Placed in the cervical opening, they serve to painlessly dilate and soften the cervix slightly. This makes dilating the cervix easier during the actual abortion.

Inserting the laminaria involves little discomfort. A speculum is inserted into the vagina as in a routine pelvic exam, and the cervix is washed with cotton swabs soaked in a special form of iodine. One or more laminaria are then inserted into the cervical opening and held in place by gauze placed in the vagina. Occasionally, women may have mild menstrual-like cramping overnight as the laminaria gently swell. The clinic or doctor usually suggests an over-the-counter pain reliever if the cramping is too distracting. The laminaria have strings attached so that they are easily removed at the time of the abortion.

## The Abortion Procedure

The abortion has two steps. First, the cervical canal has to be dilated to permit access to the uterine cavity. This is done by sliding progressively thicker metal probes through the cervix. The second step is the emptying of the uterus. This is done chiefly by a hollow plastic tube passed through the cervix and attached to a suction machine. When it is turned on, the machine makes a whirring noise that may be heard by the patient. The whole process takes about fifteen minutes.

## Pain Relief During the Abortion

General anesthesia, in which the patient is put to sleep, is rarely used. It is expensive, prolongs the recovery period, and slightly increases the risk involved with the procedure. Instead, a local anesthetic is injected directly into the cervix to block the discomfort of dilation. Some abortion clinics also provide intravenous medication. This involves placing a plastic tube into a vein in the hand so that medicine can be injected directly into the bloodstream for immediate effect. Two types of medicine are often given. A narcotic, (similar to morphine) is used to dull the pain, and a second medicine (such as Valium) is given to reduce anxiety. The combination is quite effective in helping patients through the experience without distress. Although the drugs wear off within an hour or so, the abortion clinic staff asks that the patient have someone drive her home.

## Safety

Abortions are often safe and simple procedures if performed early in the pregnancy. The chief risks of abortion are hemorrhage, infection, and damage to abdominal organs, all of which are rare. Most clinics perform a large number of abortions, and they tend to have doctors with a great deal of experience in performing the surgical procedure. They are also usually quite good in providing instructions and a twenty-four-hour number to call if problems should arise. Most gynecologists can recommend a specific facility if they do not perform this procedure.

An abortion does not affect future fertility except in extreme circumstances. For instance, numerous abortions (perhaps six or more) may tend to weaken the cervix, although even these women usually have no problem carrying to full term. Serious infection following abortion can result in infertility, but that is rare.

## Cost

An abortion performed in a clinic costs $200 to $300. When performed by a gynecologist in a hospital, it can cost between $500 and $1,000. If it is done in the second trimester, it is more expensive—between $1,000 and $3,000, depending on what is involved. Organizations, such as Planned Parenthood, can provide the service at a discount.

## After the Abortion

Most women will experience vaginal bleeding for several days after an abortion. Sometimes the bleeding can last for a week or more, but it should never be heavier than a period. Some women also have mild cramps for a day or two. Any significant pain should be reported to a physician. Women can usually return to their normal routines the day after the procedure.

Many clinics prescribe two medications for the first days following the abortion. One is to help the uterus contract so that blood loss is reduced. The other is an antibiotic to reduce the risk of infection. All medications should be taken as prescribed. Some clinics give a one-month prescription of a birth control pills to prevent another pregnancy until she sees her regular gynecologist.

In general, sex should be avoided for two weeks after an abortion. It is important to remember that pregnancy can occur again immediately, so some type of contraception should be used. Most clinics ask that the patient be examined by a gynecologist two to four weeks after the procedure to be sure that she has fully recovered.

Some women experience significant regret and depression after having an abortion. They may wonder about what the baby would have been like.

These women should see a counselor or therapist to help them cope with their emotions. Abortion is a highly traumatic experience for any woman. Even if the teens realize their decision was the right one for them, they still experience feelings of loss and depression. Counseling can help you cope with these feelings.

## The Future of Abortion

A pill readily available in France, known in the United States as Ru-486 can safely end a pregnancy without the need for any type of surgical procedure. The chemical name for Ru-486 is Mifepristone. The medication blocks the action of progesterone within the uterus. Progesterone is the hormone produced by the ovaries immediately after ovulation that sustains the pregnancy until the placenta can produce its own progesterone at about eight weeks' gestation. We know this because in the first half of the century, when surgeons removed an ovary from which an egg had been expelled during early pregnancy, a miscarriage always resulted. This progesterone is necessary for the pregnancy to continue. By blocking the action of progesterone within the uterus, Ru-486 causes the uterus to contract and expel the pregnancy.

In France, Mifepristone is taken orally as a single tablet. One to two days later a drug similar to one hormone in the group of hormones called prostaglandins is administered vaginally. Prostaglandins also cause the uterus to contract; they are sometimes used to induce labor in pregnant women. In one study of over 2,000 pregnant women, this combination of medications resulted in a rate of 96 percent for successful abortions without the need for an additional surgical procedure. The remaining 4 percent required the more traditional approach of suction curettage. One woman out of 2,115 required a blood transfusion, but otherwise there were no complications.

Ru-486 is not perfect. It must be taken under the strict supervision of a physician. It causes the patient to experience an average of nine days of vaginal bleeding. Above all, the drug must be given within seven weeks of the first day of the last menstrual period. Many women may not realize that they are pregnant, and others may have difficulty seeing a doctor soon enough.

Ru-486 is currently being tested in the United States. It has been distributed to some doctors and clinics to give to patients, but it is not widely available and has not received FDA approval yet.

# PART III
# SEXUALLY TRANSMITTED DISEASES

# What Are STDs?

More than a dozen infections are spread exclusively or primarily by sexual contact. This section discusses in detail only some of these diseases, but the underlying principles outlined in this chapter apply to all of them.

## Bacteria and Viruses

A discussion of the differences between bacteria and viruses is not the first thing you might expect to see in a book about birth control. Yet it is crucial to understanding the differences among sexually transmitted diseases. A bacterium is a single-celled microorganism that can live in our bodies. Because bacteria are actually individual cells, they have their own protective covering and can reproduce without assistance from the host they live in. As cells themselves, bacteria generally live outside of (next to) the cells or building blocks of our bodies. For that reason they are relatively easy to diagnose and treat. Generally, doctors prescribe antibiotics to treat bacterial infections. They have the virtue of killing the bacteria while not harming the patient. Examples of sexually transmitted diseases caused by bacteria include gonorrhea, chlamydia, and syphilis.

Viruses also cause a variety of STDs, but they are quite different from bacteria. It is these differences that make viruses much harder to treat. Viruses are hundreds to thousands of times smaller than bacteria and cannot function independently. They can thrive and reproduce only when physically inside body cells. Generally, the inactive virus invades the cell, takes over the cell's machinery, and causes the cell to turn out dozens or even hundreds of viral particles. Eventually the cell bursts open, releasing these viruses and thereby continuing the infection. Because the virus reproduces only when buried in a cell, scientists have found it difficult to kill the virus without killing the cell. That is why viral infections usually cannot be cured. Fortunately, the body's defenses can keep many such infections in check, but medical science usually can do little to help. Examples of STDs caused by viruses include acquired immunodeficiency syndrome (AIDS), hepatitis B, herpes, and genital warts.

## The Biology of Sexually Transmitted Diseases

By definition, these diseases are spread chiefly through sexual contact. The diseases are caused by bacteria, viruses, or other microbes that share several features. For the most part, these agents cannot survive outside of the body. They need bodily warmth and moisture found in the reproductive tract, and they can survive a transfer from one body to another only by close contact. Furthermore, these microbes cannot penetrate intact skin. They can enter the body only through breaks in the skin or the mucous membranes lining the mouth, penis, vagina, and rectum.

Another feature of the organisms that cause STDs is they usually do not cause the body to develop immunity.

With chicken pox, which is caused by a virus, the body remembers the invader and fights off all subsequent similar infections. As a result, most people can get chicken pox only once. In contrast, the body does not develop lasting immunity to the flu, and people can be infected with the same virus year after year. So it is with most of the STDs. One infection does not assure immunity. In fact, it is quite common for people with these diseases to be treated and then be reinfected a week later by the very same sexual partner.

## Facts About STDs

The following are some medical facts about STDs to help you better understand how STDs are passed from person to person.

1. An STD is always transmitted by sex unless proven otherwise. STDs exist mainly in saliva (from the mouth), semen (from the penis), and vaginal discharge (from the vagina). The exchange of any of these fluids from one person to another can cause the disease to spread. Therefore, it is possible to contract an STD from vaginal intercourse (penis to vagina), anal intercourse (penis to anus), and oral intercourse (penis to mouth or mouth to vagina). If there are cuts or sores in the mouth, an STD may even be passed through kissing.

2. You can get the same disease more than once. In fact, many people get the same disease repeatedly in the same year. If you have an STD and receive

treatment, you will get it again unless your part-
ner(s) also receives treatment.

3. You can have more than one disease at the same
time. People not only can, but often do, have more
than one disease at the same time. In one study,
one third of the women who were infected with
gonorrhea were also infected with chlamydia,
another type of bacteria. Furthermore, treatment for
one STD does not necessarily cure another STD.

4. You can have a sexually transmitted disease and
not know it. A common way many of these diseases are spread is by an asymptomatic carrier.
People with symptoms often either seek treatment
or do not feel well enough to have sex. Just
because your partner feels fine, you should not
assume that he or she is fine.

5. People may not always know they have an STD,
and even if they do, they may not tell you.
Personality and cleanliness have nothing to do with
it. Some of the nicest, best-groomed people I know
have had any variety of these diseases. One act of
intercourse with an infected partner is all that is
necessary. Bacteria and viruses have no bound-
aries. They affect people of all races, social classes,
personality types, and levels of personal hygiene.

Having sex with different people and people whom you
don't know very well can be dangerous to your health.
Your partner may or may not know he or she is infected

and may or may not tell you the truth. Since there are more than a dozen diseases and each of them is becoming more common, you take a risk any time you have sex. The more partners you have, the greater your chances of contracting an STD. Always use a condom to reduce the risks of contracting any disease and prevent pregnancy.

## The Role of Contraceptives

One of the main reasons that this discussion about STDs is included in a book about contraception is that birth control methods can reduce the likelihood that you will catch a sexually transmitted disease. Most methods of contraception provide at least a limited amount of prevention. Some methods, however, are more effective than others.

### Condom

Condoms work by preventing contact between the penis and the inside of the vagina. However it is important to remember that no method, other than abstinence is 100 percent effective. You are still risking the possibility of contracting a disease or becoming pregnant even with a condom.

### Spermicides (foams, films, creams, jellies, suppositories)

These agents inactivate or kill a variety of microbes in a laboratory setting. Their benefit during actual intercourse is uncertain, but they can provide some degree of protection.

### Diaphragm and Spermicides

Because this method involves spermicide use, it can provide some modest protection.

## IUD

This does not prevent the spread of STD. It can possibly increase the likelihood of complications due to gonorrhea or chlamydia. For this reason, this method is not often recommended for teenagers.

## Birth Control Pill

The pill does not reduce the chance of catching a disease. It may provide some protection against developing several of the more severe complications of gonorrhea.

## Condoms and Spermicides

Using a condom in combination with additional spermicide is by far the best method of preventing the spread of STDs. As noted previously, this combination also provides excellent protection against pregnancy. Of course, the only way to be assured that you will not catch an STD is to avoid having sex.

## Diagnosis of STDs

There are several basic methods for checking if someone has a sexually transmitted disease. The tests are generally quite accurate, but even if a particular test fails to turn up the offending bacterium or virus, it is still possible that you may have the disease.

## Physical Examination

For some diseases, such as gonorrhea and chlamydia, direct examination can sometimes increase the doctor's suspicion of disease, but the doctor cannot be certain without specific testing. In contrast, an attack of genital herpes can often look so distinctive that the doctor can be sure it is herpes without any further testing.

A physical examination can be helpful in diagnosing herpes, syphilis, AIDS, and genital warts. It is not as helpful in identifying gonorrhea and chlamydia with certainty.

## Culture

This method involves swabbing the appropriate body part with a cotton swab and then touching the swab to a specially designed bacterial or viral nutrient. The test tube or petri dish containing the sample is then incubated in the laboratory at body temperature for several days. During this time, the bacteria or viruses, if present, grow in large numbers and their accumulation eventually becomes visible. If the typical changes occur in the test tube, it becomes easy to identify the microbe. On the other hand, if no growth occurs we may not know whether it is because no bacteria are present or because something is wrong with the nutrient.

The culture technique is helpful in identifying gonorrhea and chlamydia. It can also be used for herpes when there is uncertainty on examination. It is not commonly used for diagnosing AIDS, syphilis, or genital warts.

## Tissue Scraping

This test involves gently scraping a suspicious sore and placing the scrapings on a slide for examination under magnification. In this way it is possible to diagnose syphilis, herpes, or genital warts on the cervix. The technique is not very popular because it often fails to diagnose disease that other methods would normally pick up.

A Pap smear can also detect both warts on the cervix and precancerous changes. It is important to realize that the Pap smear is imprecise and that one normal test does not prove beyond doubt that a cervix is normal. That is one reason why it is so important for sexually active women to have a Pap smear and general exam at least once a year. Cervical problems are unlikely if yearly Pap smears continue to show up as normal.

## Protein tests

Proteins are molecules that provide the structure, support, and even the so-called machine parts for individual cells. They are a vital component of all living things, including humans, bacteria, and viruses. Proteins unique to a specific living organism are called antigens. For example, specific bacteria have special antigens that are not found anywhere else. Their presence in bodily fluids or in the bloodstream can be used to diagnose certain diseases. It is this technique that is used to test for syphilis and, in recent years, chlamydia. In the case of syphilis, a blood sample is obtained from the patient and tested for the presence of a syphilis antigen. For chlamydia, the cervix is swabbed and the mucus obtained is specially stained. If the antigens unique to chlamydia are present, they become visible as colored spots.

Another type of protein test is one that detects the presence of antibodies. An antibody is a protein produced by the body in an effort to defend itself against specific foreign invaders. The presence of these antibodies in the bloodstream indicates either past or present infection by a particular bacterium or virus. This is the type of screening test used with HIV, the virus that causes AIDS. It is not the virus itself that is detected, but rather the body's response to it in the form of antibodies.

## Biopsy

A biopsy is the removal of tissue from a living being for further examination. The tissue removed is stained and examined under the microscope. It is not used commonly to diagnose sexually transmitted diseases, although it is almost always used to diagnose cancer. The one exception is that a biopsy is often performed to prove the diagnosis of genital warts, particularly on the cervix. On the cervix they are not as obvious as on the outside of the body, and a small piece of tissue is sometimes taken to prove the diagnosis. Since the cervix has few nerves, the removal of a tiny piece of tissue does not normally hurt.

## Summary

No single test can prove that a person is free of disease. In fact, each sexually transmitted disease has its specific own test. Furthermore, many of these tests cannot prove the absence of disease; they are often more useful in proving only its presence. Most of the tests do not reveal any disease if the onset of the infection was very recent. In other words, the disease may require a waiting period before it can be identified by a test procedure. That is because the microbe has to reproduce to be present in detectable amounts.

# Specific Diseases

More than a dozen sexually transmitted diseases exist. According to health experts, more than 55 million people in the United States carry some type of STD. Many are unaware they have a disease. The discussion here is limited to those diseases that are notorious and widely feared that are very common and have significant medical implications.

## AIDS

AIDS stands for acquired immunodeficiency syndrome and is caused by the human immunodeficiency virus or HIV. HIV affects both sexes as well as people of any race, religion, and age. Although there have been recent advancements in the treatment of AIDS, there is no cure. When HIV enters the body, it attacks the body's immune system and weakens it. Over time the immune system may be weakened to a point that it can no longer fight off illnesses. Simple illnesses, such as a cold or the flu, which a healthy immune system can normally fight off, can be deadly to someone with HIV.

Having an STD increases a person's chances of contacting HIV. Many STDs cause sores or other wounds that allow HIV easy entrance into the body.

## How Is HIV Transmitted?

HIV can only be passed from person to person through the exchange of blood, semen, or vaginal fluids. Activities in which these fluids can be exchanged include having unprotected sex (having sex without using a condom) with an infected person or sharing dirty needles. Women who have been infected by the virus can also pass it on to their babies during vaginal delivery or through breast milk. Before 1985 people were also affected through blood transfusions when they received blood from infected individuals. However, it is now standard practice to carefully screen and test the blood supply.

You cannot get HIV from hugging someone, shaking someone's hands, eating food prepared by an infected person, or even kissing someone.

## Testing for HIV

The HIV test is a simple blood test that detects HIV antibodies in your bloodstream. The presence of these antibodies indicates that the virus is present because the body has launched these antibodies in an attempt to stop the virus.

It usually takes the body six months to produce enough antibodies to show up on a test. If you have had unsafe sex, you need to wait six months before being tested. If your body has not had enough time to produce enough antibodies to be detected by the test, your test may indicate you are HIV-negative, when you are actually HIV-positive.

## What Happens After HIV?

A person who is HIV-positive does not necessarily have AIDS. People infected with the virus can be healthy, live active lives, and not experience any symptoms of AIDS at all. However, as the virus spreads throughout the body, it weakens the body and breaks down the immune system. Early symptoms include fatigue, fever, diarrhea, enlarged lymph nodes, loss of appetite, or night sweats. As the virus progresses, these symptoms can increase and the body is further weakened until it can no longer fight off simple illnesses. Fungal infections, rare types of pneumonia, several forms of cancer, and extreme weight loss are just some of the health problems that indicate the onset of AIDS.

It takes an average of ten years for an HIV-positive person to develop AIDS. Virtually all HIV-positive people will develop AIDS, but with treatment, the onset of AIDS can be delayed.

## Syphilis

About 43,000 new cases of syphilis were reported in the United States in 1995. According to the World Health Organization, an estimated 3.5 million people worldwide have infectious syphilis.

### What Is It?
Syphilis is an infection caused by the bacterium Treponema pallidum. Under the microscope the microbe looks like a corkscrew. It cannot survive outside the body for more than a few minutes, and it is transmitted almost exclusively by sexual intercourse.

### What Are the Symptoms?
The answer to that question is neither simple nor straightforward. Syphilis has three stages, each with its own symptoms.

## Primary Syphilis

This is the appearance of a chancre, or sore, ten to ninety days after intercourse with an infected partner. The sore is a break in the skin surface and is firm, painless, and smooth. There may be more than one such sore. The chancre marks the site of bacteria entry into the body and therefore is usually on or close to the genitals. It may occur in hard-to-see locations, such as the vagina or mouth and can last from two to eight weeks.

## Secondary Syphilis

Six weeks or so after chancre appears, the person becomes ill with fever, muscle aches, and any one of a variety of skin rashes. A rash that appears on the palms of the hands or the soles of the feet may be considered syphilis by a physician until proven to be otherwise. The illness and rash are only temporary and disappear even without treatment.

## Tertiary Syphilis

Only one-third of those initially infected and untreated develop tertiary syphilis. This stage occurs years or even decades after the initial infection. Treponema pallidum can reproduce in various organs. When it reproduces in the heart and great blood vessels the structures are weakened, and ultimately the patient dies when the vessels burst. If it reproduces in the brain, the person becomes insane. In fact, before penicillin, syphilis was one of the major causes of insanity.

## Diagnosis and Treatment

Although some of the symptoms of syphilis are unique,

the diagnosis can be confirmed with an inexpensive blood test. Syphilis at any stage responds readily to antibiotics, although in its third stage it can do significant damage if not recognized early enough.

## Gonorrhea

A bacterial infection of the reproductive organs in either sex, gonorrhea is caused by the bacteria Neisseria gonorrhoeae. An estimated 1 million people contracted gonorrhea in 1995.

### Symptoms

Many people who contract this disease never know it. Twenty years ago most men who had the disease experienced extreme burning during urination. Over the course of years, the illness has changed so that now only about half of infected men have a discharge or burning with urination. Women are even less likely to have symptoms. Their symptoms can include a heavy vaginal discharge or pain on urination; but these are common symptoms in women, and they are only rarely due to gonorrhea. The usual time span from infection to visible symptom appearance is one to fourteen days.

Gonorrhea can also infect the throat and rectum, depending on one's sexual practices. At either site, it can cause pain. If a rectal infection occurs, rectal bleeding may be one of the symptoms.

### Complications of Gonorrhea

The complications that can result from gonorrhea make

this common infection a serious one. While one percent of patients develop widespread, infectious arthritis, this complication is less common than PID.

PID occurs when bacteria invade the normally germ-free uterus and fallopian tubes of a woman. Although this serious infection can be caused by several bacteria, gonorrhea is one of the chief culprits. Gonorrhea can ravage the internal reproductive organs and damage the body's defenses so that normally harmless bacteria in the vagina can cause further damage. The symptoms of PID and the damage that it causes occur because many other bacteria overrun the body after the initial assault by gonorrhea.

The symptoms of PID are highly variable. The infection can be a silent one, destroying the fragile fallopian tubes without a woman ever feeling ill. The symptoms can range from mild menstrual-like cramping to a dull ache in the pelvis. Alternatively, the patient can become quite ill with unbearable abdominal pain, nausea, vomiting, and high fever. PID is treatable with antibiotics. The chief concern is that 10 percent of women with their first infection have irreversible damage to the fallopian tubes. These women have less than a 50 percent chance of becoming pregnant even with intensive, expensive medical treatment.

### Diagnosis and Treatment of Gonorrhea

The chief method of diagnosing gonorrhea is by bacterial culture. A suspected site of infection is touched with a swab, which is then smeared onto bacterial nutrients. A negative culture does not prove that a person does not have gonorrhea because the bacteria are very picky about their growing conditions. Of ten people with known infections, the culture method proves the diagnosis in nine.

Diagnosing PID is much more difficult. By the time a woman is sick enough to consult a doctor, the gonorrhea bacteria have often been overrun and replaced by other bacteria. Pelvic inflammatory disease is diagnosed by excluding other causes of pain and fever.

Gonorrhea is treatable with antibiotics, either in the form of pills or shots. If a person is known to have gonorrhea, all of his or her sexual partners should be treated immediately, whether or not it can be proved that they have the infection. If they are not so treated, they can infect other sexual partners.

## Chlamydia

This disease is caused by a bacterium similar to the one that causes gonorrhea. It is becoming more and more widespread and probably infects more than one million people in the United States. According to the Center for Disease Control and Prevention, an estimated 4 million people were infected in 1995.

Chlamydia causes the same symptoms (or absence of symptoms) as gonorrhea does. It too is a leading cause of PID. In one study, one-third of college women who had gonorrhea also had chlamydia. As a result, everyone who has gonorrhea is also automatically treated for chlamydia.

The standard test for chlamydia involves a culture. A new test that specifically identifies proteins unique to chlamydia in bodily secretions is fast replacing the culture technique. This method is painless; the cervix or penis is touched with a special swab and the swab smeared onto a slide.

A new antibiotic called azithromycin can cure chlamydia, and it takes only one injection to do so.

# Herpes

Thirty-one million people are believed to be infected with herpes, and 500,000 new cases were reported in 1995. Herpes can cause pain and suffering for brief episodes, but it does not cause lasting bodily damage or death as can many of the other STDs. One exception to this comment, discussed below, is that a mother's active herpes infection can infect her newborn and make the baby seriously ill.

## Symptoms

The symptoms of herpes should be divided into two groups: those that occur with the first episode and those that occur later. It is important to realize that some people with herpes can be contagious between outbreaks.

In those who do have symptoms, the first episode or outbreak is usually the most severe. In the typical case, extremely painful blisters appear on the genitals, accompanied by flu-like symptoms. Many people have a high fever, muscle aches, and even nausea. The entire episode usually lasts between ten and fourteen days. Of those who have one attack, 20 percent never have another outbreak.

For the majority who have repeated episodes, the episodes can occur every several years or as frequently as every several weeks. The subsequent outbreaks are much less severe. In most cases, the blisters are somewhat less painful and are present for a shorter period of time. It is unusual to develop flu-like symptoms. For most people, a herpes infection results in a few week-long episodes of painful blisters per year.

### Diagnosis of Herpes

For those who have suspicious symptoms, there are two main methods of diagnosis. The first, examination by the doctor, can often establish a herpes infection without any testing. For those who have the characteristic blisters, simple examination of the sores is often accurate in confirming the diagnosis.

When there is doubt, a culture of the blisters can be done. The culture technique involves swabbing a blister vigorously so that the fluid it contains spills onto the tip of the swab. The swab is then placed in a solution that contains nutrients for the herpes virus and incubated for at least a week. If herpes is present, characteristic changes will be detected. It may take as long as seven days for the virus to make itself evident. A culture cannot be read as negative until after the full week.

A positive culture for herpes is rarely wrong; however, the culture technique cannot be used to prove the absence of herpes, since the virus might not grow well in the laboratory even if present. Also, the virus is present in the blisters only for a short time. If the culture is taken too early or too late (after the blisters have started to heal) a positive culture is less likely even if the blisters truly are from herpes.

### Complications

Genital herpes has few complications other than self-limited episodes of discomfort. It does not shorten life, nor does it cause damage to body organs or protracted illness. One exception is that babies born to mothers who have a herpes outbreak at the time they go into labor can contract the infection and become seriously ill. As a result, these babies are often delivered by Caesarean section to reduce the chance that they will contract the virus from direct contact with the blisters.

## Treatment

The first episode of herpes can be curtailed and made less severe by the use of acyclovir tablets. The brand name for acyclovir is Zovirax. In subsequent episodes, however, Zovirax is of little or no benefit.

Zovirax can be used to reduce the frequency of attacks. If three to five tablets are taken every day, the majority of patients will have far fewer episodes. Once the Zovirax is stopped, the frequency of attacks often picks up again. Once another outbreak occurs, Zovirax is of little benefit.

## Genital Warts

The symptoms of genital warts are not very noticeable, even when they are identified by a doctor during a physical examination. Despite its inconspicuousness, the wart virus is not harmless; it is now thought to be a significant cause of cervical cancer.

## Symptoms

These warts are usually small and painless. Sometimes they are so small that they cannot be seen without a microscope. As a result, physicians are often the first to notice that a patient has them. Men and women may be aware that they have a wart on their genitals but not realize that it is contagious and should be treated.

Genital warts large enough to be seen look like any other warts. Usually, they are flesh-colored irregular bumps. They may exist only internally, particularly in women, and thus be undetectable by the patient.

## Diagnosis of Genital Warts

Diagnosis is by simple inspection and by biopsy. When there is doubt, the doctor can take a small piece of tissue from the suspected area for special staining and microscopic examination.

In women, warts on the cervix are sometimes detected by a Pap smear, which is usually recommended once a year. If the Pap smear suggests that warts exist, a follow-up microscopic exam is suggested, allowing the doctor to see the cervix close up and biopsy any suspicious areas. The outside area can also be inspected under magnification since the warts there may be too small to see. A normal Pap smear does not prove that a cervix is normal, nor does an abnormal Pap smear prove that warts are present.

In men, the penis is dabbed with diluted vinegar and then examined with a microscope or a magnifying glass. The vinegar helps any suspicious area stand out from normal tissue.

## Complications

Some strains of the wart virus (human papilloma virus) can cause cervical cancer if ignored over several years. If the wart is close to the anus it may also have a role in the development of anal cancer, although this disease is uncommon, even in those who have warts.

## Treatment of Genital Warts

With persistence, genital warts can usually be eliminated, although several treatments may be required. Warts on the outside can be burned off with a laser or a cautery device, removed by a knife, or eliminated through the use of special chemicals. Usually, injections of local anesthetic are used if the warts are to be burned or cut off. The chemical methods may sting a little but usually are not too uncomfortable. Warts on the cervix can also be frozen, a remarkably fast and easy process with little discomfort. After treatment, the patient should make a follow-up visit to be checked for any further occurrences. Women with cervical warts need frequent Pap smears to be sure that treatment was completely successful.

## STDs and Pregnancy

Most of the sexually transmitted diseases discussed in this chapter pose a significant threat to a developing fetus or a newborn. The impact of each of these diseases on the newborn is briefly reviewed below.

### AIDS

One in four babies born to mothers infected with HIV also contract the virus. Mothers can also pass the virus to their babies through breast milk. Babies who contract the virus usually don't live to adulthood.

### Syphilis

Miscarriages and stillbirths are the most common results of pregnancy in mothers who have syphilis. For those babies born in spite of it and not treated, complications include bone deformities, heart damage, and deafness.

### Gonorrhea
Many decades ago, gonorrhea was a leading cause of blindness among newborns. In modern times, all newborns be treated within an hour of birth with eye drops that kill the bacteria if they are present.

### Chlamydia
This disease can also cause blindness in newborns. Eye drops are available that kill both gonorrhea and chlamydia so that neither has a chance to damage an infant's eyesight.

### Herpes
The herpes virus can threaten a baby in two ways. If a pregnant woman becomes sick with herpes for the first time, the infection can cause miscarriage, stillbirth, or severe damage to the baby. It is unusual, however, for a woman to contract herpes for the first time while she happens to be pregnant. A more common problem is the threat posed by repeated attacks of herpes. These is some chance that a baby born during an episode will acquire the infection from direct exposure to the sores. Such a newborn has a significant chance of death or brain damage from a severe infection. As a result, women who have an outbreak of herpes during labor are often delivered by Caesarean section to prevent any contact between the baby and the open genital sores.

## Genital Warts

As a rule, this infection poses the least threat to a newborn baby. In fact, the only complication that can occur is that the baby could get warts on the vocal cords, in which case the newborn would eventually become hoarse. This is quite uncommon and easily treatable, and no special precautions need to be taken by pregnant women with genital warts. Apart from the well-being of the baby, the mother's warts tend to be more difficult to get rid of while she is pregnant.

Teenagers who engage in sex with numerous partners need to be aware of the consequences of their behavior. In order to stay healthy you need to be careful about your sexual partners. Better yet, keep to one partner, or still better, abstain completely. But if you choose to have sex, always use a condom.

# PART IV
# QUESTIONS AND
# ANSWERS ABOUT SEX

# Frequently Asked Questions

## Contraception

1. Is continuous use of the pill dangerous?

No. There is no evidence to suggest that continuous use of the pill for years poses any sort of unique danger. People who go for long periods of time without having sex and who are using the pill solely for contraception probably should go off the pill when they are not sexually active. However, there is no reason why one cannot stay on the pill for twenty or more consecutive years.

2. I heard that the pill causes cancer. Does it?

No. Not only does the pill not increase the risk of any type of cancer, but it is thought to decrease the chances of developing ovarian and uterine cancer.

3. My boyfriend refuses to use birth control, and I do not want to go on the pill. What should I do?

Find a new boyfriend or abstain from sex. Although the pill is a safe and effective form of birth control, many women do not wish to use it for a variety of reasons. I suggest that spermicides not be used alone, although they are reasonably reliable and much better than nothing. If the diaphragm is not acceptable to the couple, the only remaining contraceptive is the condom. Also, remember that the condom provides protection against STDs, such as AIDS.

If the only option is a condom and the male refuses to use it, a woman has two courses of action. She can end their relationship (and find a more reasonable partner) or simply abstain. No woman should ever become pregnant simply because her partner refused to wear a condom.

4. Will the birth control pill make me gain weight?

Not usually. The medical literature suggests that for every woman who gains weight on the pill, another loses weight. A very few patients may gain ten to twenty pounds on the pill, but with more than a thousand pill prescriptions in my practice every year, I cannot remember a single person who gained that much weight as a result of oral contraceptives. In fact, when patients have complained of gaining weight, more often than not their recollection of what they weighed and when does not reflect the written, dated record in their charts. Most people have a five- to ten-pound weight variation over the course of a year. Since many people start the pill when they want to be intimate with a new boyfriend, weight may simply be affected by the lifestyle changes that often accompany a new relationship.

5. Will the pill help my PMS?

When my patients ask this question, they are usually talking about cyclic irritability. Although no treatment or medication is known to significantly improve irritability in the majority of people, some of my patients report an improvement once they start the pill. Of course, others complain that the pill worsens their moodiness. The pill may have a variable effect on PMS irritability, but most patients do not seem to notice much of a difference one way or the other.

6. Should I take a break from the pill?

No—not unless you wish to become pregnant. In fact, it is common for women who take a break from the pill to accidentally get pregnant. There is a widely held but false idea among the lay population that there is some health benefit to stopping the pill temporarily after taking it for a number of years. This is simply not true. The pill remains a safe option for continuous use beginning in the teen years at least to the age of forty in nonsmokers and age thirty-five in smokers.

7. How far in advance should I stop the pill before trying to get pregnant?

Of course, this whole book is based on the premise that teens should not get pregnant. For older women who are planning to become pregnant, we generally recommend going off the pill and using

barrier methods of contraception (such as the condom) for three months before trying to conceive.
The pill is not strongly suspected to cause birth
defects, and women who accidentally become
pregnant while taking the pill usually have healthy
babies. The advice to stop three months in advance
is to allow menstrual periods to resume sponta-
neously and to reduce the chance of having twins.
Women who conceive within three months of stopping the pill have a slightly increased chance of
having twins.

8. What if a condom breaks?

Used correctly, a condom almost never breaks. It
should be used only once, and space should be left
at the end of the penis to hold the semen. If the
condom does break there is not much you can do
about it after the fact. Prevention is the best treatment. Remember not to douche in an effort to wash
the sperm out, as this might only force some of
them higher into the vagina.

9. What if my period is late and my pregnancy test is
negative?

A home pregnancy test is usually quite accurate as
long as a woman's menstrual periods are fairly regular and it is done when the period is truly overdue. Missing a period when you're on birth control
pills is different from missing a period when you're
not on the pill. If a sexually active woman who is
taking the pill correctly misses her period, she

should simply start the next package of pills as she normally would. If she misses two periods in a row, she should first do a home pregnancy test and then call her doctor. A doctor may suggest that she change pill brands so that she can resume having regular periods and thereby be reassured that she is not pregnant.

A sexually active woman who misses her period and is not on the pill needs to follow a different plan. If the first home pregnancy test is negative, she should wait one to two weeks and repeat it. If the second test is also negative, a doctor should be consulted. Frequently a medication will be prescribed to bring on a period if it is more than a few weeks past due.

## Sexually Transmitted Diseases

1. Can you get an STD from a toilet seat or bathtub?

No. All the microbes commonly transmitted by sex are killed very quickly (within minutes) at room temperature and by soap. Further, in sharing a bath with someone, the bath water dilutes any surviving organism to such low concentrations that disease transmission is virtually impossible.

To catch a disease from a toilet seat, you would have to sit on the seat immediately (within one or two minutes) after a person who had an open, draining sore that could deposit fluid on the seat.

You would have to have an open wound yourself that would come in direct contact with that fluid. Finally, the skin in contact with the toilet seat is not the penis or the vaginal opening but rather the back of the thighs—a very unusual place for sores and breaks in the skin.

2 Can you have an STD and not know it?

Yes. In fact, many people do. It is common for people to be infected with HIV, syphilis, gonorrhea, chlamydia, and genital warts without realizing it. On the other hand, it is relatively unusual to be infected with herpes without knowing it.

3. I was just told by my doctor that I have genital warts. I have had only one boyfriend for two years. Does this mean that he must have been playing around?

No. Sexually transmitted diseases do not incubate over a precise time period. The doctor can seldom tell how long the disease has been present or where the patient got it. Proving that a disease is present is always easier than proving that it is absent. Particularly in the case of genital warts, the human papilloma virus can be present for a long time in either partner without their realizing it.

4. How can I avoid getting herpes?

Use condoms and additional spermicide with every episode of intercourse, although this is by no means absolute protection. Be sure about your partner's sexual history. If you suspect you have herpes and have had unprotected sex, you should see your doctor for proper testing.

You should remember that herpes is actually the least dangerous and important of all the common sexually transmitted diseases. Its only significant health threat is to an infant born during a period when the mother's herpes is active.

5. What is chlamydia?

This is an infectious disease transmitted through sexual intercourse and caused by bacterium Chlamydia trachomitis. It has many similarities to gonorrhea in that it can cause (a) stinging on urination, (b) a vaginal discharge, and (c) sterility in women.

6. I have a bad-smelling vaginal discharge. Is that a sign of an STD?

Not usually. Although some of the more serious sexually transmitted diseases, such as gonorrhea or chlamydia, can cause a discharge, most discharges come from something else. Specifically, several different microbes cause self-limited vaginal infections. Although some of these organisms can be transmitted through sex, they are not a threat to health and are treated merely because they cause annoying symptoms.

Women who notice that their vaginal discharges have a powerful odor should see a gynecologist so that the appropriate medication can be prescribed and the condition can be corrected. Rarely, the doctor may actually suspect the presence of a significant sexually transmitted disease and will order the necessary tests.

7. How can I avoid getting AIDS?

The answer is exactly the same as for avoiding herpes. The use of condoms and limiting the number of sexual partners is a way to keep this risk to a minimum. The best way is to practice abstinence. Also, as with herpes, if you have had unprotected sex and suspect you may have contracted HIV, you need to see your doctor immediately for proper testing.

# Sexual Knowledge
## Self-Test

This is a twenty-question true-or-false and multiple-choice test designed to help you check your knowledge of important facts. Answer the following questions on a separate sheet of paper. All the answers are contained somewhere in the book (including the last chapter). They should be easy to find and study. The answer key follows the test.

### TRUE/FALSE

1. A female must be at least eleven years old before she can become pregnant.

2. A man or woman may have a sexually transmitted disease and not know it.

3. A pregnant woman with a sexually transmitted disease can pass the STD on to her baby.

4. A sexually transmitted disease may result in sterilization.

5. Masturbation or self-stimulation is harmful and abnormal.

6. It is physically harmful for men and women to stop sexual activity short of intercourse.

7. It is more difficult for a man to stop sexual activity short of intercourse than a woman.

8. A woman will not conceive if the man does not climax during intercourse.

9. A woman will not conceive if she does not have a climax during intercourse.

10. Pelvic inflammatory disease (PID) is often a complication of gonorrhea in women.

## MULTIPLE CHOICE

Choose the one best answer.

11. Which of the following provides the most effective birth control?

A. Condom

B. Diaphragm and spermicide

C. Pill

D. IUD

12. Which of the following is most useful in preventing the spread of a sexually transmitted disease?

A. Condom

B. Rhythm Method

C. Pill

D. IUD

13. Pain on urination may mean that a sexually

active male could have:

A. Syphilis

B. Gonorrhea

C. AIDS

D. Genital warts

14. All of the following statements about menstrual periods are true except:

A. The menstrual flow consists of blood and an unfertilized egg.

B. It can occur with backache, cramping, and moodiness or with no discomfort at all.

C. It is most likely for a woman to get pregnant if she has sex during menstrual period.

D. The total amount of blood loss during a woman's period is a few ounces.

15. About how many young woman out of 100 become pregnant if they have sex on a regular basis for one year and do not use contraception?

A. 25 percent

B. 50 percent

C. 80 percent

D. 100 percent

16. At what point in the menstrual cycle is a woman most likely to become pregnant if she has sexual intercourse?

A. One or two days before her period begins.

B. One or two days after her period begins.

C. During her period.

D. Midway between her periods.

17. What is the minimum number of times a woman must have sexual intercourse to become pregnant?

A. One

B. Two

C. Three

D. Five

18. Which of the following statements is false?

A. A sexually transmitted disease refers to a disease spread exclusively by sexual contact.

B. Condoms and spermicides may be useful in preventing the spread of sexually transmitted disease.

C. Once treated and cured, a person will never get the same type of sexually transmitted disease again.

D. One can have several different types of sexually transmitted diseases at the same time.

19. Abstinence refers to:

A. Not having sexual contact.

B. A specific type of sexually transmitted disease.

C. Sexually immature males and females.

D. Having sexual contact with only one partner.

20. A wet dream or nocturnal emission:

A. Means that a boy or girl has wet the bed while sleeping.

B. Occurs when a man ejaculates during his sleep.

C. Is an abnormal symptom.

D. Refers to sweating while dreaming about sex.

21. Which disease is most likely to impair female fertility?
A. Syphilis
B. Herpes
C. Genital warts
D. Chlamydia

22. Select the one true statement about AIDS:

A. Condoms provide protection against AIDS.

B. It is a disease that only male homosexuals get.

C. A person can carry the virus that causes AIDS for years before getting sick.

D. You can catch it from toilet seats.

23. Which contraceptive does not require a doctor's prescription?
A. Diaphragm
B. Birth control pill
C. IUD
D. Condom

## ANSWER KEY

| | |
|---|---|
| 1. False. | 13. B |
| 2. True. | 14. C |
| 3. True. | 15. C |
| 4. True. | 16. D |
| 5. False. | 17. A |
| 6. False. | 18. C |
| 7. False. | 19. A |
| 8. False. | 20. B |
| 9. False. | 21. D |
| 10. True. | 22. C |
| 11. C | 23. D |
| 12. A | |

# Glossary

**abortion**  Medical procedure that terminates a pregnancy.

**abstinence**  No sex.

**anesthetic**  A drug that numbs a particular area of the body so that a person doesn't feel any pain.

**antibody**  A protein the body produces to fight off specific foreign invaders.

**biopsy**  The removal of tissue from a living being for further testing.

**cervix**  Opening of the uterus.

**contraception**  Devices or methods that prevent a pregnancy from occurring.

**douche**  To wash or rinse out the vagina with a liquid.

**ejaculate**  For men, to have an orgasm, to "come."

**fallopian tubes**  Organs that connect the uterus to the ovaries.

**fertilize**  To create life, to begin pregnancy.

**fetus**  Developing baby.

**gynecologist**  A doctor who specializes in the care of the reproductive organs of females.

**hymen**  A thin membrane surrounding the vaginal opening which usually tears during first sexual intercourse.

**labia**  Lips of the vagina.

**menopause**  The end of a woman's fertility; the complete ending of her periods.

**menstrual cycle**  Female monthly bleeding in which the body sheds its uterine lining and unfertilized egg.

**obstetrician**  A doctor who specializes in the care of pregnancy and birth.

**orgasm**  The climax of sexual stimulation, known as "coming."

**ovaries**  Organs in the female body that produce eggs.

**ovulation**  The release of an egg from the ovaries.

**Pap smear**  A test that involves taking a tissue sample from a woman's cervix and testing it for abnormalities.

**speculum**  An instrument used to separate a woman's vaginal walls during pelvic exams.

**STD**  Sexually transmitted disease.

**uterus**  Organ in a female's body in which a baby develop. and receives its nourishment.

**withdrawal**  A poor method of birth control in which the male removes his penis from the vagina just before ejaculation.

# Where to Go for Help

American Health Foundation
320 East 43rd Street
New York, NY 10017
(410) 859-1500

National AIDS Hot Line
(800) 342-2437

National Organization on Adolescent Pregnancy and
    Parenting, Inc. (NOAPP)
4421-A East-West Highway
Bethesda, MD 20814
(301) 913-0378

National Teen Pregnancy Clock
Web site: http://www.cfoc.clock.html

National Youth Crisis Hot Line
(800) 448-4663

Planned Parenthood Federation of America
810 Seventh Ave.
New York, NY 10019
Web site: http://www.ppfa.org/ppga/
(800) 230-7526

Sexuality Information and Education Council of the United
States (SIECUS)
130 West 42nd St.
New York, NY 10036
(212) 879-1990

Teen AIDS Information
(800) 234-TEEN

Women's Healthline
(212) 230-1111

Teen Pregnancy and Prevention and Intervention Program
Web site: http://goldmine.cde.ca.gov/www/lsp/teenhome.html

# For Further Reading

Ayer, Eleanor. *It's Okay to Say No: Choosing Sexual Abstinence.* New York: Rosen Publishing Group, 1997.

Boston Women's Health Book Collective. *The New Our Bodies, Ourselves.* New York: Simon & Schuster, 1992.

Bullough, Vern L. *Contraception: A Guide on Birth Control Methods.* Buffalo, NY: Prometheus Books, 1997.

Carrol, Janell L. and Paul Root Wolpe. *Sexuality and Gender in Society.* New York: HarperCollins, 1996.

Harlap, Susan. *Preventing Pregnancy, Protecting Health: A New Look at Birth Control Choices in the U.S.* New York: Alan Guttmacher Institute, 1994.

Mucciolo, Gary. *Everything You Need to Know About Birth Control.* New York: The Rosen Publishing Group, 1997.

Nourse, Alan Edward. *A Teen Guide to Birth Control.* New York: Franklin Watts, 1988.

————. *Sexually Transmitted Diseases.* New York: Franklin Watts, 1992.

Pasquale, Samuel A., and Cadoff, Jennifer. *The Birth Control*

*Book: A Complete Guide to Your Contraceptive Options.*
New York: Ballantine Books, 1996
Simpson, Carolyn. *Coping with an Unplanned Pregnancy.*
New York: The Rosen Publishing Group, 1996.
Woods, Samuel G. *Everything You Need to Know About STD.*
New York: The Rosen Publishing Group, 1997.
Zinner, Stephen. *How to Protect Yourself from STDs.* New
York: Summit Books, 1986.

# Index

## A

abortion, 77–83,
  cost of, 80–81
  numerous, 80
  pain relief during, 79–80
  safety of, 80
abstinence
  periodic, 35, 34–37
  total, 35–36, 109, 116
acne, 19, 36
acquired immunodeficiency
      syndrome (AIDS),
  86, 91, 93, 94, 95–96, 119,
      121
  and pregnancy, 105
  symptoms of, 96
acyclovir, 103
Advil, 12
alcohol
  in pregnancy, 27
anemia, 46
antibody, 92–93, 95
antigen, 92
arousal, sexual, 7
arthritis
  infectious, 99
  rheumatoid, 47

## B

baby
  and AIDS, 105
  calculating due date of, 26
  and chlamydia, 121
  development of, 10, 28
  and genital warts, 121
  and gonorrhea, 106
  and herpes, 101, 103, 106,
      121,
  and syphilis, 105, 121
bacteria and viruses, 85–86, 91,
      92
basal body temperature (BBT),
      37
benefit, health
  of abstinence, 36
  of contraceptives, 53–54
  of diaphragm, 72
  of Norplant, 50
  of the pill, 46
  of spermicides, 75
biopsy, 93
birth defects, 62
bladder, 10
bleeding
  in first trimester, 25

irregular, 43–44, 45–46, 52, 56
rectal, 98
reduced, 46
vaginal, 11, 14, 17, 25, 40–41, 81, 83
blisters, herpes, 101–103
blood
menstrual, 11, 14, 31
transfusion, 95
breast, 28
budding, 19
milk, 95

**C**

calendar technique, 36–38
cancer, 96
anal, 104
cervical, 22, 104
protection against, 47
cervical canal, 10
cervical cap, 73
cervical mucus, 37, 40
cervical warts, 105
cervix, 10, 21, 22, 59, 71, 73, 78, 79, 80, 92, 93, 105
precancerous changes of, 22, 92
chancre, spyhilitic, 97
chlamydia, 61, 90, 92, 100–101, 121
and pregnancy, 121
similarities to gonorrhea, 100
symptoms and testing, 100
treatment of, 101
Chlamydia trachomitis, 115
circumcision, 8

clitoris, 9
condom, 30, 31, 59, 65–68, 90, 95, 121
cost of, 68
effectiveness, 66–67
with spermicide, 74, 75–76
contraception, 32
choice of, 30–32
effectiveness of, 31–33, 51, 57, 59, 64, 65, 66–67, 72–73, 79
hormonal, 55–57
safety of, 30–31, 50, 60
and STDs, 31, 32
Cowper's glands, 8
cramps, menstrual, 46
curretage, 83
cyst, ovarian, 46–47

**D**

Depo-Provera, 55–56
depression, 44, 56, 81–82
development
female, 19–20
male, 18–19
diaphragm, 67, 69–73, 90, 118
effectiveness of, 73
insertion of, 70–72
removal of, 72
safety of, 72–73
douching, 33, 35
abuse abuse, 27

**E**

egg
fertilized, 25
unfertilized, 10, 11, 14, 15

ejaculation, 7, 8, 19, 35, 67
endometrium, 10, 11
epididymis, 7
erection, 8, 66
estrogen, 14, 50, 51,
examination
  bi-manual, 21
  gynecologic, 20–22
  for STDs, 90–91

**F**
fallopian tubes, 10, 14, 61, 62, 99
fertility
  female, 11, 14–19, 20, 51, 80
  male, 19
film, vaginal, 74–75
follicle, 14
follicular phase, 15
foreskin, 8

**G**
genitals, 36, 97, 101, 105
glans, 8
gonorrhea, 61, 90, 92–100, 118, 119
  and chlamydia, 100
  complications of, 98–99
  diagnosis of, 99–100
  and pregnancy, 119
  symptoms of, 98
  treatment of, 99–100
Grafenberg ring, 58
gynecologic exam, 20–22

**H**
hepatitis B, 86

herpes, 36, 86, 91, 101–103, 121
  and babies, 101, 103–104
  complications of, 113
  diagnosis of, 102
  and pregnancy, 116
  symptoms of, 101–102
  treatment of, 103
high blood pressure, 55
hormones
  female, 12, 14, 51, 59, 82, 91
  synthetic, 52, 55
human immunodeficiency virus (HIV), 93, 94–96
human papilloma virus, 114
hygiene, feminine, 13–14
hymen, 9

**I**
ibuprofen, 12, 61
infection
  Norplant, 52
  pelvic, 61
  rectal, 98
  STD, 86–87
  viral, 93
infertility, 61
intercourse
  anal, 87
  oral, 87
  pain in, 9
  sexual, 2, 3, 8, 25, 34, 35, 38, 56, 64, 67, 96, 114, 116, 120
IUD, 35, 56–64, 99
  effectiveness of, 59
  history of, 58

and pregnancy, 62–63
risks of, 59–60
safety of, 60–62
and teens, 63

## J
jelly, spermicidal, 71, 89

## L
labia
  majora, 8, 9
  minora, 8
laminaria, 78–79
luteal phase, 15

## M
Marker, Russell, 39–40
masturbation, 36, 115
Mefipristone, 82
menopause, 12
menses, 12, 14, 43, 59
menstrual cycle, 11–17
menstrual flow, 11, 46

## N
nausea,12, 24, 44, 72, 56, 99,
  101
Neisseria gonorrhoeae, 98
Norplant contraception, 50
  benefits of, 50
  disadvantages of, 51–52
  insertion procedure of, 53–54
  removal procedure of, 54
  risks of, 52
  safety and effectiveness of,
    50–51

side effects of, 52–53

## O
orgasm, 6, 38, 66
ovaries, 10, 20, 38, 40, 82
ovulation, 12, 14, 34, 40, 44,
  46, 54, 82
  detection kit, 37
  predicting, 17, 37, 38
  prevention of, 40, 50

## P
pain
  in abortion, 79–80
  menstrual, 12–13
  mid-cycle, 54
  pelvic, 15, 60
  on urination, 98, 114, 188
Pap smear, 20, 21, 22, 90, 91,
  104
Paragard, 58
partners, sexual,
  multiple, 61, 86, 106
pelvic inflammatory disease
  (PID), 46, 60, 96, 98
  and chlamydia, 60, 63
  and gonorrhea, 46, 60, 61, 63
penicillin, 97
penis, 6, 8, 34, 38, 64, 66, 86,
  88, 100, 104, 112
period, menstrual, 10, 12, 14,
  16, 18, 20, 22, 24, 26,
  37, 40, 41, 45, 50, 54,
  59, 72, 112, 118
  absence of, 20, 24, 51
  charting, 37
  first, 12, 19, 20

irregular, 24, 51
overdue, 24, 25
pill
  abortion, 82–83
  birth control, 31, 32, 38, 39,
    108
  forgetting, 43
  generic, 49
  health benefits of, 46–47
  health risks of, 47–48
  morning-after, 56
  and PMS, 111
  Progestin-only, 55
  side effects of, 44–46
  starting, 41–43
  stopping, 43–44, 111
placenta, 28, 82
posterior fourchette, 9
pregnancy, 24–28,
  avoiding, 24
  chance of, 17, 20, 24
  duration of, 26
  ectopic, 62–63
  medical care and, 26–27
  signs of, 24–25
  and STDs, 105–107
  teenage, 4, 28,
  tests, 24–25
premenstrual syndrome (PMS),
    111
primary syphilis, 97
progesterone, 115, 39, 40, 52,
    82
progestin, injectable, 33
prostaglandins, 12, 82
prostate gland, 7

puberty, 18, 19, 20
pubic hair, 8, 19, 72

R
rectum, 21, 86, 98
rhythm method, 36
risks, health
  of abortion, 80
  of diaphragm, 72–73
  of IUD, 60–62
  of the pill, 47–48
  of Norplant, 52
  of spermicides, 75
Roe vs. Wade, 77
Ru-486, 82–83

S
sanitary napkin, 13
scrotum, 7
secondary syphilis, 97
semen, 6, 35, 87, 95, 112
seminal vesicles, 8
sex
  premarital, 37
  teenage, 3, 28
sexually-transmitted disease
    (STD), 3, 30, 32, 65, 75,
    76, 85
  biology of, 86–87
  and contraceptives, 89–90
  diagnosis of, 90–93
  facts about, 87, 89
  and pregnancy, 105–107
side-effects
  of Norplant, 52–53
  of the pill, 44–46

smoking
  and the pill, 48
speculum, 21
sperm, 16, 38, 96, 70, 71
  production of, 8
spermicide, 68, 74–76
  condom and, 68, 76
  diaphragm and, 70
  effectiveness of, 75
  safety of, 75
sterility, 115
suppository, spermicidal, 74
symptoms
  of chlamydia, 100
  of genital warts, 104
  of gonorrhea, 98
  of herpes, 101–102
  menstrual symptoms, 12–13
  of ovulation, 17
  of PID, 61
  of pregnancy, 24
  of syphilis, 96–97
syphilis, 96
  diagnosis of, 97–98
  pregnancy and, 105–106
  symptoms of, 96–97
  treatment of, 97–98

T
tampon, 13, 14, 72
tertiary syphilis, 97
test, diagnostic
  bacterial culture, 99, 102
  blood, 78, 95, 98
  HIV, 95
  protein, 92–93
  tissue scraping, 91–92, 104

viral culture, 102
testicles, 7, 8, 19
toxic shock syndrome (TSS),
  14, 72
Treponema pallidum, 96
ultrasound, 29, 87

U
urethra, 8, 9
uterus, 10, 11, 12, 15, 16, 22,
  69, 72, 87, 109

V
vagina, 8, 9, 11, 13, 14, 17,
  35, 36, 38, 59, 61, 65,
  70, 71, 72, 73, 74, 75,
  78, 86, 87, 89, 97, 99,
  112
vaginal discharge, 130, 131
vaginismus, 37
vas deferens, 7
virginity, 37
  loss off, 14, 33, 78, 121

W
warts, cervical 115
warts, genital, 38, 95, 100,
  113–115, 129, 130
  complications of, 115
  diagnosis of, 114
  pregnancy and, 117
  symptoms of, 114
  treatment of, 115
weight gain,
  and the pill, 51, 125
  in pregnancy, 28, 29
wet dream, 20

withdrawal, 35, 36, 45,
        121–122
womb, 10, 22, 29, 69, 70

## Z

Zovirax, 113